C O N

M000094753

INTRODUCTION

"Toto, I've a feeling we're not in Kansas anymore." Like Dorothy, I had a feeling I wasn't in New Orleans anymore. I was in my new home, Washington, D.C., directing a film crew on the steps of the United States Senate. After a few pleasantries with our on-camera client, Senator J. Bennett Johnston, we were ready to roll.

In those days, my director's ensemble consisted of a tuxedo shirt, embroidered jacket with tigers front and back, pressed and creased jeans, tennis shoes – and above the neck: beard, permed hair and Elton John glasses. I don't recall who said it. Must have been one of the Senator's people. "Who's the guy in costume?" As Curly of the Three Stooges used to say, "I resemble that remark!"

My DC friends told me to tone it down a little. They said politicians are serious people, and besides, this wasn't Hollywood, so I ditched the jacket. But what I refused to ditch were the two motivating forces in my writing – humor and satire.

As the new kid on the block, I wasn't getting much business, so I tried some new marketing approaches. I sent Matt Reese, a big shot political consultant, a six-inch piece of loose video tape with a note reading, "Enclosed is a piece of my work. If you'd like to see more, please call."

I got a call from Reese, who said, "I didn't get the joke until I asked somebody in the office. They said it was funny so come on over." Reese gave me a ton of business.

Other prospective clients got mannequin legs stamped with, "We won't charge you an arm and a leg for good production." None of those people called. Maybe it was too grotesque.

This book contains descriptions and scripts from some of

my favorite ads and videos using humor and satire – powerful weapons in political advertising. Studies have shown that humorous TV ads have a higher rate of recall and are more persuasive. Psychologist Carol Moog offered this theory to the *New York Times*: "Humor gives people a way to vicariously express their aggression. It reaches them above the base consumer level. It appeals to their intellect, and makes them feel bright." Hopefully, you'll feel bright after reading this book.

In my ads and videos, I've used a dead fish as a prop and a 2,000 pound Brahman bull as an actor. I've also used chickens, pigs, horses, goats, a camel, a 1949 Mercury, a kazoo band, women on drugs, professional wrestlers, floating hamburgers, a funeral hearse, scantily clad showgirls – whatever it took to get people's attention, amuse them, inform them and get them to vote for my candidate or against the opponent. Currently, we're introducing humor and satire into an American political arena lacking both creativity and civility.

In addition to candidate campaigns, I've included ads and videos from other related projects – advocacy, lobbying, public service, tax policy, healthcare, animal welfare, utility regulation, labor relations, agriculture, gaming, food and nutrition. The last chapter, Salon des Refusés, features scripts that were rejected by the client and never produced. (All are copyrighted, adaptable and available for purchase and production. Operators are standing by.)

If you'd like to see some of the ads described in this book, please go to denoseder.com.

1

VOTE FOR DUKE.
CREATE A FÜHRER.

David Duke flew under the radar. The pollsters' antennae failed to detect the covert candidate's true range or velocity. Evil was flying low, scavenging for votes like a vulture.

People would not admit they were planning to vote for the former Grand Dragon of the Ku Klux Klan. Were these voters too embarrassed to tell the truth? Were they ashamed? Ignorant? Racist? High on meth? Perhaps a combination thereof.

In 1990, Duke ran for the U.S. Senate in Louisiana against incumbent Senator Bennett Johnston. My firm was hired to develop a campaign strategy and TV ads for a third-party group, The Louisiana Coalition Against Racism and Nazism. I relished the idea of running a campaign against Duke. Our paths had crossed years earlier when, as a graduate student at LSU, I heard this fair-haired freshman rant about white supremacy, a Jewish one-world conspiracy, and other racist rubbish. At the time, I dismissed him as an unpleasant anachronism. And an asshole.

David Duke was not only a former Klansman, he was also a neo-Nazi. In 1979, he traded his hood and robe for a Brooks Brothers suit, ran for the state legislature and won by only seventy-two votes out of more than 16,000 cast. He served one term, during which he was caught selling, with shameless audacity, Nazi books and tapes from the basement of his legislative office.

1

Lance Hill, a professor of history at Tulane, served as director of the Louisiana Coalition. "We wanted to defend the principles of equality and justice in the face of Duke's assaults. We wanted to appeal to the moral conscience of voters." But Lance became increasingly discouraged during the course of the campaign. "Voters first response to the truth about Duke was defensive. To admit that he was a fraud and a racist was to admit that they were being misled or were bigots. People don't like to admit this. We were holding a mirror up to the electorate and telling them that they and David Duke were one and the same." And sadly, tragically, many of them were.

One week before the election, polls showed Johnston with over 60 percent of the vote and Duke at 26 percent. Johnston's own pollster, Geoff Garin, showed his client at 65 percent. A *Times-Picayune* headline read, "Johnston a virtual shoo-in, analysts say." But the analysts had been wrong before, and I started feeling a simmering trepidation about becoming the media guy who lost to David Duke.

On election night, Duke shocked the state and the nation. He got 43.5 percent of the vote to Johnston's 54 percent. Nearly 60 percent of white people voted for Duke, and he beat Johnston in virtually all working-class white neighborhoods and rural areas. The victory party at Bennett Johnston's hotel ballroom was a somber, muted affair.

The following year, emboldened by his strong showing in the Senate race, Duke announced he would run against incumbent Governor Buddy Roemer. Nine other candidates were also on the ballot, including former Governor Edwin Edwards. Three days before the primary election, a Mason-Dixon poll showed Roemer at 31 percent, Edwards at 30 percent and Duke at 22 percent. Five local pollsters also predicted Roemer to run first, followed by Edwards and then Duke. The final results were:

DEAD FISH

Edwin Edwards	33.8%
David Duke	31.7%
Buddy Roemer	26.5%

I was on a plane the next day to New Orleans to help Lance Hill and the Coalition gear up for another fight. A massive voter registration effort was begun. Within three days of the election, 68,000 Louisianans registered to vote. More than half of them were black. On October 22, 1991, the last day to register for the November 16 runoff, the lines of people waiting to register were often two and three blocks long. In the town of Gretna, for example, more than 2,000 people were still in line at 8:00 p.m. when the courthouse office was supposed to close. Many of them had been waiting in line for five hours, and most of them were black. The office stayed open until after midnight to make sure everyone was able to register. The same scenario played out all across the state. Democracy in action! The historic Louisiana registration drive made the evening news on all the major TV networks.

Edwards had a reputation as a ladies man and was having fun with Duke. He told a reporter, "The only place David Duke and I are alike is we're both wizards under the sheets." And this gem: "Duke will never be governor of Louisiana and the swastika will never replace the pelican" [the state bird].

A Mason-Dixon poll came out a few days after the primary showing Edwards leading Duke, 46 to 42 with only 12 percent undecided. Of that 12 percent, 10 were white and 2 were black. We had to stop this guy. With my partner and co-producer (my son Jeorge), we started writing scripts and producing ads at a furious pace. We decided to hit him hard on his affinity for one of history's most malevolent mass murderers.

Adolph Hitler's hagiographer was Leni Riefenstahl, a German filmmaker. The Führer loved her sycophantic

3

cinematography. Jeorge and I wrote and produced a spot using footage from Riefenstahl's *Triumph of the Will,* a shocking and surreal 1934 propaganda documentary which glorified Hitler and the Third Reich with creepy black and white images of Nazi pomp and pageantry. For a soundtrack, we added a grandiose theme from the virulent ant-Semite and Hitler favorite, Richard Wagner.

"Nazi" 30-sec. TV

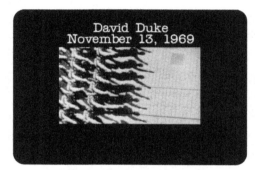

(Music: Wagner – "Flight of the Valkyries")

(VO) In 1969, David Duke said, "I am a National Socialist. You can call me a Nazi if you wish."

In 1976, he organized a meeting of a Nazi group

which called for the release of all Nazi war criminals.

In 1988, he hired

a former American Nazi Party captain

to manage his presidential campaign.

And in 1989, David Duke was caught selling Nazi books and tapes

from the basement of his legislative office.

(Crowd) Seig heil! Seig heil!

This dark and chilling satire may have pulled some votes away from Duke, but the *coup de grâce* was a parody of the game show *Jeopardy*, which we called *Jabberwocky*, the title of a lovely nonsense poem by Lewis Carroll.

We shot the 60-second ad in a Washington, D.C. studio. It featured four professional actors, a custom-built game show set, and was shot with three cameras. Since the ad parodied the *Jeopardy* show, we created five categories: Tax Cheats, Crazy Ideas, False Patriots, Good Buddies and Basement Booksellers. The response to each category was "Who is David Duke?" Here are the script and still frames:

"Jabberwocky" 60-sec. TV

(Music and applause)

(Host) Thank you and welcome back to Jabberwocky,

the game show all America loves to watch.

Bill, Alan and Debbie, are you ready?

(Bill, Alan and Debbie) Ready!

(Host) Debbie, you first.

(Debbie) I'll try False Patriots for three hundred please.

(Host) He was kicked out of ROTC, lied about serving his country

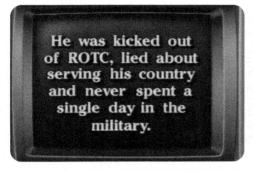

and never spent a single day in the military.

(FX buzzer)

(Debbie) Who is David Duke?

(Host) Correct!

(Debbie) Good Buddies for three hundred.

(Host) He hired ex-Nazis to work on his political campaigns.

(FX buzzer)

(Host) Bill

(Bill) Who is David Duke?

(Host) Yes!

(Bill) Paul, I'll try Tax Cheats for two hundred.

(Host) He failed to file state income taxes from 1984 to 1987.

(FX buzzer)

(Host) Alan

(Alan) Who is David Duke?

(Host) That's right!

(Alan) Crazy Ideas for four hundred Paul.

(Host) He has advocated that America be divided into separate race nations.

(FX buzzer)

(Host) Debbie

(Debbie) Who is David Duke!

(Host) Right again, Debbie!

(Debbie) Basement Booksellers for three hundred.

(Host) He says he's changed his ways, but just last year he was caught selling Nazi books and tapes

from the basement of his legislative office.

(FX buzzer)

(Host) Alan

(Alan) Who is David Duke?

(Host) Yes!

(FX bell)

(Host) And that's the end of round two. Stay tuned folks, we'll be right back.

In his book, *Winning Elections, Campaign Management, Strategy & Tactics,* Ron Faucheaux wrote: "*Jabberwocky* worked beyond all expectations. In addition to exposure through paid media, it got extensive coverage in Louisiana and national media outlets. Duke was thrown on the defensive, and his momentum blunted." I started feeling better about our chances to stop this neophyte Nazi.

Duke was getting national visibility apart from our ad. *The New York Times* ran several articles about the race, and Duke was making appearances on network evening news and talk shows including *Good Morning America, Nightwatch, Larry King Live, Crossfire and Today.* The talking heads weren't kind to Duke, but as P.T. Barnum used to say, "There is no such thing as bad publicity." And like a clown in a circus, Duke loved the spotlight.

Our ad was having an effect, not only was it getting votes, but it was raising money, especially from Hollywood. We got checks from Dustin Hoffman, Michelle Pfeiffer, Dan Akroyd, James Garner, Norman Lear, Herb Alpert and many others. In appreciation, every donor was sent an air sickness bag with Duke's photo on it and the words, "David Duke makes me puke."

On election night, at precisely 8:00 p.m. when the polls closed, Bob Schieffer came on the air with a "CBS News Special Report." Based on exit polls, Schieffer said, "Edwin

Edwards has been elected governor of Louisiana over David
Duke by a substantial margin." The final results were:

| Edwin Edwards | 61% |
| David Duke | 39% |

The *Associated Press* wrote, "Cheers for the defeat of David
Duke sounded in New Orleans and across the nation Saturday
night." An uncharacteristically calm Lance Hill told a reporter,
"I think Louisiana redeemed itself. This isn't so much a defeat
of a political candidate, but a triumph of decency and
compassion."

I like to think that our satirical ads helped in that triumph.

The following year, *Jabberwocky* won a Clio Award, the
Oscar of the advertising industry. Meanwhile, David Duke
crawled back under his rock until Donald Trump came along
and said it was ok to come out.

2

WE DON'T
ALWAYS AGREE.

It was my first trip to Orlando. During the cab ride from the airport to the hotel, I imagined how Jim Carrey's character in *The Truman Show* must have felt living in the artificial TV utopian bubble of his hometown, Seahaven. Everything about Orlando is pristine and manicured. It feels prefabricated. Every palm frond is deep green and unspoiled. An abundance of artfully arranged small lakes and ponds adorn the lush landscape. Fifty million tourists visit the city and its more than a dozen theme parks every year, including Disney World.

But I didn't come to Orlando to meet Mickey. I came to help save 6,000 dogs. Greyhound dogs. Eleven of the seventeen remaining greyhound race tracks in America are in Florida. This "sport" is cruel and inhumane. Every three days a dog dies on a track in Florida. They die from broken necks, broken backs, cardiac arrest, electrocution and euthanasia. The dogs are confined in small cages for up to twenty-three hours a day. They're given steroids, fed raw meat from diseased animals, and in a ten-year period, sixty-eight greyhounds were tested positive for cocaine, novocaine, lidocaine, oxycodone, oxymorphone and the industrial solvent DMSO.

Grey2K USA Worldwide is a wonderful nonprofit organization in Boston whose mission is to pass stronger greyhound protection legislation and to end the cruelty of dog racing on both the national and international levels. In June of 2018, I got a call from Carey Theil and Christine Dorchak, who head up the organization, asking if I would like to help them pass an amendment in Florida to ban dog racing. We had worked together in the past to ban dog racing in Massachusetts, so I was familiar with the issue, and ready to go to work.

Amendment 13 on the 2018 Florida ballot, if passed, would phase out this barbaric spectacle. Carey and Christine explained that the Florida legislature had created a hurdle for ballot initiatives, i.e., they need sixty percent of the vote to pass.

The Florida ballot listed multiple local and statewide candidates, U.S. House and Senate candidates, and thirteen ballot measures. Amendment 13 was the very last measure. When voters don't understand a ballot measure's language, they will often skip it or vote no. They get tired, frustrated, and when voter fatigue sets in, apathy follows.

The Orlando Hyatt Regency is a massive resort hotel with several pools, shops and restaurants, 24-hour spas, the whole deal. (The veggie burger in the hotel's funky retro diner was excellent.) The plan was to assemble a video crew and interview a dozen or so supporters of Amendment 13. From my interviews, we would edit 30-second TV ads as well as longer pieces for social media and distribution to news outlets.

The people we interviewed were great. They were all enthusiastic animal welfare advocates including a veterinarian, a five-year-old girl and two elected state officials.

One ad, "People," featured twelve supporters of Amendment 13 and was the primary ad that ran on broadcast television. It was a big hit. Another ad, "Mike and Carlos," featured two Florida State Representatives, conservative Republican Mike Hill and liberal Democrat Carlos Smith. Mike was a six-foot, two-inch, square-jawed, no-nonsense kind of guy. Carlos was much shorter, stylishly dressed, gregarious and witty. We had Carlos stand on a box to bring him within a few inches of Mike. This was the first time these two had come together on any issue, and while I sensed some awkwardness, it was not palpable.

We wanted to inject a little humor in the ad, and the guys were ready. Mike would be the stone-faced straight man. Carlos would play it a little looser, and after a few takes, they nailed it.

"Mike and Carlos" 30-sec. TV

(Mike) I'm a Republican.

(Carlos) I'm a Democrat.

(Mike) We don't always agree.

(Carlos) You can say that again.

(Mike) We don't always agree.

(Carlos) Except on this issue.

(Mike) We're both voting yes on Amendment 13.

(Carlos) Because we both agree…

(Mike) That greyhound dog racing is cruel and inhumane.

(Carlos) Every three days a greyhound dog dies in Florida.

(Mike) From cardiac arrest, broken necks, broken legs.

Carlos) But together…

(Mike) Republicans…

(Carlos) and Democrats…

(Mike) We can phase out this cruel spectacle.

(Carlos) Agreed?

(Mike) Agreed.

(VO) At last, something we can all agree on.

Vote yes on Amendment 13.

Mike and Carlos soon became cult heroes on the internet, and in a state rife with partisan rancor, they were a breath of fresh air.

The opposition, meanwhile, was hammering away at our side on social media. They called us animal rights extremists, accused us of wanting to outlaw hunting and fishing (the NRA gave them $900,000) and tried to assure the Florida voting public that "greyhounds were born to run" and that the dogs were being treated with loving care. What bullshit. One toady for the greyhound dog racing industry, I'll call him Joe Bob, was making crude videos attacking us while professing his love for the dogs. The videos begged, no screamed, for a satirical response. And respond we did:

"Joe Bob" 50-sec. Video

(Dog racing supporter) They're dogs, they're not people.

(VO) Greyhound dogs deserve to be treated humanely.

(Dog racing supporter) And it's not because they've been abused, know what I mean?

(VO) No we don't know what you mean,

because every three days

a greyhound dies

on a racetrack in Florida.

(Dog racing supporter) They love more than anything to chase that fake rabbit around the track.

(VO) How do you know what dogs love?

Do they love being confined in a small cage for 20 to 23 hours a day?

(Dog racing supporter) I mean where else do you get to go, have some fun and hang out with your friends, right?

(VO) Maybe you think it's fun,

but 70 percent of Florida voters oppose greyhound racing.

(Dog racing supporter) That's greyhounds man, they got it made.

(VO) No they don't. A Florida state government report stated that

confining these animals in cages was

"cruel,

inhumane

and abusive."

(Dog track supporter) They're dogs, they're not people.

(VO) And in November,

the people will protect the dogs.

Stop the cruelty.

Vote YES on
Amendment 13.

The opponents' tactical strategy gave us a great opportunity to counterpunch with continued satire and ridicule.

The campaign strategy Carey and Christine came up with was simple and smart – raise as much money as you can and put ninety percent of it in TV placement. And it worked. The ballot measure passed with sixty-nine percent.

3

WILD ABOUT HARRY

Harry Lee was an improbable hero. The nation's first Chinese-American sheriff had become the most popular elected official in Louisiana. And maybe the largest. A conspicuously corpulent 350 pounds, Harry sang on stage with Willie Nelson, partied at the White House with pal Bill Clinton, used his political power to raise big money, most of which he gave to charity, and while fighting crime in the largest parish in Louisiana, elevated political incorrectness to high art.

Harry was a client and a friend for twenty-eight years. New Orleans political writer Clancy DuBos once commented, "They say never say never in politics, but there will never, ever be another politician like Harry Lee."

In his foreword to my biography about Harry, President Clinton wrote:

> "I was amazed to learn that after getting elected five times, Harry had earned an approval rating of nearly 90%, the highest in the state and maybe even the nation. In the world of politics, that's almost unheard of."

Also unheard of was a politician who trusted his media consultant enough to let him do whatever he wanted.

In 1978, Harry first ran for sheriff of Jefferson Parish against a firmly entrenched, albeit shady, incumbent. Polls revealed that Harry was virtually unknown, had a vote total of less than five percent, and as a Chinese-American Democrat in a Republican parish, would not be politically palatable. My

27

kind of candidate.

Huey Long popularized Louisiana politics as a spectator sport. His approach to government was to "find out what people want and give it to them." The Long mythology, resplendent with inflammatory rhetoric and overwrought populism, wasn't a good model for Harry, but there was something about his obliging style and populist inclination that was appealing. What was not appealing, however, was his ethnicity. We knew that a lot of voters simply would not relate to the idea of a Chinese sheriff.

Our first ad for Harry featured him with his wife, Lai, and daughter Cynthia, walking along the Mississippi River levee, while the requisite resonant voice-over narrator talked about him and his qualifications. Harry asked that we select his wardrobe for the shoot. While rummaging through his closet, my co-producer, Dorothy Kutiper, spotted a Stetson cowboy hat on the shelf and learned that Harry wore this on hunting trips. "Wear the hat, Bubba," I told him, "and the blue denim jacket and cowboy boots."

The hat was a hit. The *Times-Picayune* wrote, "It should have been ludicrous. But instead, the image of Harry Lee as an Oriental cowboy apparently became the chance find of all the Jefferson campaigns." And Clancy DuBos wrote in *Gambit Weekly*, "When he made the cowboy commercial, that's when things took off. He seemed so incongruous, yet so American." A few weeks later, I saw the Chinese cowboy on a stage with a band at a pig roast singing country songs. The crowd loved it. I loved it, and couldn't help but think of the Willie Nelson song, "My Heroes Have Always Been Cowboys."

The incumbent sheriff, Al Cronvich, had been convicted of illegal wiretapping, and had resigned from office, only to come back and run again. Wire tapping was no big deal among the electorate, until we made it a big deal, without ever mentioning the specific crime:

"Al" 30-sec. TV

(Al Cronvich on camera)

(Cronvich) I am a man of integrity.

(Freeze frame)

(VO) On April 19th of this year, Al Cronvich was indicted by a grand jury for knowingly and intentionally violating the law.

(Cronvich) I am a man of integrity.

(Freeze frame)

(VO) On June 14th, he was convicted.

(Cronvich) I am a man of integrity.

(Freeze frame)

(VO) On July 11th, he was sentenced.

(Cronvich) I am a man of integrity.

(Freeze frame)

(VO) And on July 14th, he announced his candidacy for sheriff of Jefferson Parish.

(Cronvich, with echo) I am a man of integrity.

(Freeze frame, fade to black and super)

Harry Lee, Sheriff

Harry Lee was elected sheriff of Jefferson Parish on December 9, 1979 with fifty-three percent of the vote. On the same day, Jack Singletary was elected police juror in Vernon Parish in west Louisiana. Singletary had died six weeks before the election. I love Louisiana politics.

Harry's first election may have been his easiest election. Eight years later, a formidable challenger, Art Lentini, pulled a Willie Horton, attacking Harry for allowing a jailed rapist to serve as a trusty in a program designed to let inmates perform certain tasks assigned by the sheriff. The local press jumped all over Harry. The *Times-Picayune* demanded his immediate resignation, calling him "manifestly unfit...cavalier...flamboyant...overbearing." A columnist for the paper predicted "Lee is dead in the water, apparently sunk by Brian Busby [the convict]."

In a field of three candidates, Harry was forced into a runoff. A week after the primary election, the University of New Orleans released a poll:

Lentini	50%
Lee	30%
Undecided	20%

Things looked bleak. Loyola political science professor S. J. Makielski remarked, "Losers have a smell and winners have a smell, and Lee is beginning to smell like a loser." Harry confessed to his family and campaign team that he was considering resigning. But Harry's close friend and confidant, Marion Edwards, chided him for his attitude: "Look Harry, you did absolutely nothing in the primary. It's time to go to work!"

I made a series of attack ads blasting our opponent, a former prosecutor, for his predisposition toward plea bargaining. The strongest ad opens on a small ice cream cone with a red flashing custom-made neon sign in the background – "Mr. Softee." The camera zooms in to reveal moving footage of the opponent's face in the ice cream. The film was shot in time lapse, causing the ice cream to melt, drip and make a mess. Discordant calliope music accompanies the announcer:

"Mr. Softee" 30-sec. TV

(calliope music)

(VO) It's Mr. Softee,

former Assistant D.A. Art Lentini.

He talks tough but has a soft heart, especially when prosecuting criminals.

In his last two years as an Assistant D.A.,

Mr. Softee tried only eight jury trials

while plea bargaining 135 others.

He agreed to reduce the charges in 135 cases, including three murders and four aggravated rapes.

As a crime fighter, Art Lentini, Mr. Softee, has made a mess.

The freakish visage of our opponent in the melting ice cream cone was indelible, and the charges against him, indefensible. Harry was re-elected sheriff with fifty-four percent of the vote.

Subsequent elections were much easier, and the ads even wackier. One featured three ladies from a senior home, wearing identical red dresses, singing "I'm Just Wild About Harry" in a high kitsch set (white latticework covered with artificial flowers, glittery curtains, neon stars and clouds, and bubbles, lots of bubbles (remember Lawrence Welk?).

"Wild About Harry" 30-sec. TV

(music and vocal) I'm just wild about Harry, and Harry's wild about me.

The heavenly blisses of his kisses fill me with ecstasy.

He's sweet like chocolate candy and like honey from a bee.

Oh I'm just wild about Harry, and Harry's wild about me.

(VO) The people of Jefferson Parish are wild about Harry

and Harry's wild about them.

But that's not surprising because together,

they've made Jefferson Parish a safe place to live, work and raise a family.

Re-elect Harry Lee,
Sheriff.

And they did. Harry won re-election with seventy-two percent of the vote in a field of four candidates.

Harry's popularity was, once again, soaring. He would be Sheriff-for-life. But in 1995, he surprised everyone and announced he would run for governor. A poll showed Harry in a four-way statistical tie for second place in a field of fourteen candidates. But few of Harry's friends, including me, liked this idea. We weren't sure if his heart was really in it, and we reminded him of the grueling physical and emotional demands of a statewide campaign.

In any event, we supported him.

Gambit Weekly wrote, "He is definitely the candidate people are talking about. And chances are he will stay that way." Greg O'Brien, Chancellor of the University of New Orleans, told me in an interview, "Harry was somebody everybody in the state could relate to. They related to him because they saw somebody who shared their values, an honest guy that they could have faith in, and yet somebody who really knew how to get things done. They felt he was always there for them."

Eight weeks later, realizing that this wasn't what he really wanted, Harry withdrew from the race. He loved the people of Jefferson Parish and they loved him, but he wasn't finding love on the campaign trail. He told me, "I don't think I was running to see if I could be governor, but to see if a poor kid born in the back room of a Chinese laundry could be governor."

Harry could have won this election, but we'll never know. I do know this, however - we had fun trying. Here are a few of the ads I made for him:

"Dinner" 30-sec. TV

(Harry Lee) I've been a judge, a parish attorney, a general

and for the last fifteen years, I've been a sheriff.

And then some reporter says I'm too fat to be governor. Adding insult to injury,

a friend said that when I ride in a parade, people stand and cheer, for the horse.

Well I've got news for you guys, I've lost seventy pounds and I'm running for governor.

I'm going to fight crime and make Louisiana safe, just like I have in Jefferson Parish.

(FX: dinner bell)

(VO woman) Harry, dinner!

(Harry Lee) I'll be right back.

Another spot opened on a large antique cotton scale with a five-foot platform and three-foot diameter dial. The scale was positioned in front of the State Capitol in Baton Rouge. Candidate look-alikes took turns stepping up on the scale, got weighed, and then stepped down. The camera cut to a close-up of the dial to show the weight of each candidate. Harry was the last candidate to get weighed. He tipped the scale at over 280 pounds. This was the narration for the gubernatorial weigh-in:

"He's No Lightweight" 30-sec. TV

(VO) As the candidates for governor weigh in, one this is clear –

when it comes to fighting crime,

these contenders are lightweights.

Crime is the number one issue in Louisiana,

and these candidates want you to believe

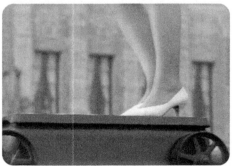

their tough talk

will stop violent criminals.

It won't.

There is only one
candidate for governor

with a proven record
for putting criminals
where they belong –

Harry Lee.

When it comes to fighting crime,

he's no lightweight.

Harry Lee, Governor.

At a New Orleans political fund raising event in April, 2000, the keynote speaker, President Bill Clinton was joking about how he came to be impeached. He turned to Harry and said:

"And I want to thank my good friend, Sheriff Harry Lee, who proved to me that you could get bad press and the people would stay with you. [laughter and applause] So I simply decided to test the theory and it got a little out of hand. [laughter and applause] Now that's a crack I probably wouldn't make anywhere in America, outside of Louisiana." [laughter and applause]

Honestly, I don't think I've had as much fun playing politics anywhere in America, outside of Louisiana.

4

BULL

Steeped in a vat of vainglory, the campaign slogan is meant to crystallize the persona, vision, values and whatever of a candidate. Nixon's the One. It's Morning in America. Compassionate Conservatism. Change We Need. Yes We Can. I'm with Her. Make America Great Again.

In the 1979 Louisiana governor's race, with more than a dozen candidates running, it was hard to match the slogans with the man. (There were no women running.) The slogans were trite and trivial (Louisiana First, I'm nobody's man but yours) although my favorite was this memorable monostich for Louisiana House Speaker, E. L. "Bubba" Henry:

Hubba, hubba, vote for Bubba.

The *Washington Post* wrote, "During the last eight months, six major candidates for governor, and their image-makers, have waged the longest, most intensive television campaign this state – perhaps any state – has seen. They will have spent an estimated $20 million, or about $10 per registered voter – more than has ever been spent in an election in a single state." That record would be broken fours years later. (See Chapter 5, "My Way").

The *Post* also quoted an old friend, Dr. Ed Renwick, a Loyola University political scientist and pollster: "Politics are entertainment here. It's a sport. The governor's race is a Super Bowl of politics. The governor is almost a constitutional dictator.

45

The amount of money in contracts and patronage he controls is incredible." And the amount of money spent on consultants was incredible. During this election, the media consultants included Jimmy Carter's filmmaker Robert Squires, Washington-based consultant Mark Shields, and Academy Award-winning filmmaker Charles Guggenheim, among others.

One of the candidates vying to become the next constitutional dictator was my client, State Senator Edgar "Sonny" Mouton. In his book, *The Last Hayride*, John Maginnis described Mouton as "...one of the most brilliant and effective legislators ever and a man who waxed more eloquent in debate and more crafty in strategy with every hit of Stolichnaya he had from the pint bottle he carried with him in the chamber."

Our polls showed Mouton in sixth place among the six major candidates. A weak sixth place. We had to act quickly, strategically, and creatively.

I read the 30-second TV script to Mouton. He laughed. The next step was to find the four-legged on-camera talent.

At the time, I was living in New Orleans. I called a friend who had a farm across the river in Bossier Parish. "Hey Buddy (Buddy Roemer, who would become a congressman and governor) you got a bull I can borrow for a TV commercial?" Three days later, Buddy's sister, Melanie, delivered a 2,000 Brahman bull to the KSLA TV studio.

Jeff Kimble (Mission Impossible, Top Gun, etc.) was flown in from Los Angeles to be the cinematographer. Since we didn't have a smoke or fog machine to create a textured atmosphere, Jeff suggested we spread some straw on the studio floor, dampen it slightly, and then burn it so it smolders.

The finished spot got a lot of publicity, locally and nationally. The *Washington Post* wrote, "Across the picture of a large, white-faced bull flashed the slogans of other candidates. After the last slogan came a voice: "Tired of the same old bull?

Vote for Edgar Mouton."

The backstory of this production, however, was fraught with calamity and hilarity. The bull was not fond of smoke. After several takes, he got spooked, became irritable and knocked over a light, which caused a small fire and mild panic. Melanie somehow wrangled the bull out of the studio, while someone ran and got a fire extinguisher. Minutes later, a fire truck arrived and dowsed the entire studio, creating even more smoke. It was 9:45 p.m. and the news crew came in to set up for the ten o'clock news. They were not happy. We watched the news from the green room. There was a lot of texture in the air. So much texture that the news anchors couldn't read their teleprompters.

Oh, by the way, our bull spot was a resounding success. Mouton went from a weak sixth place to a strong sixth place.

"Bull" 30-sec. TV

(Instrumental: America the Beautiful)

(VO reads campaign slogans of opposing candidates)

Leadership is the difference.

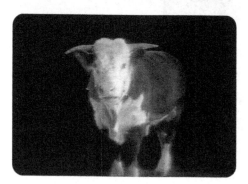

Louisiana first.

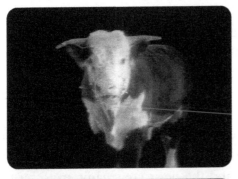

I'm the only candidate who is tough on crime.

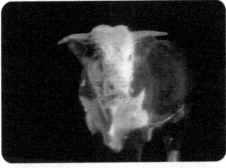

Together, we can make a difference.

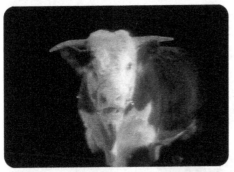

I'm nobody's man but yours.

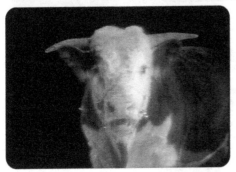

(Bull bellows)
(VO) Tired of the same old bull?

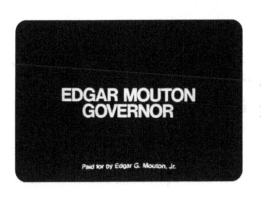

Vote for Edgar Mouton, Governor.

5

MY WAY

Four years after we nearly burned down a television station in Shreveport, Louisiana, I got a phone call from Victoria Edwards, daughter of the former governor, Edwin Edwards. She asked if I would like to make a pitch to "the Governor" to serve as his media consultant and producer.

In Louisiana, a governor cannot serve more than two consecutive terms, but can run as often as he or she wished. Edwards served four terms as governor. This time, he was running against the incumbent, Dave Treen, the first Republican governor since Reconstruction. Edwards told a reporter, "He's so slow it takes him an hour and a half to watch "60 Minutes." I figured if this guy has a sense of humor, he might like my style.

Political observer John Maginnis characterized Treen as a man who "failed as a politician to present a clear vision of what he wanted to achieve, to point the direction in which he was going and marshal resources to get the job done…stern and wooden."

Victoria scheduled an appointment with Edwards and told me I would have fifteen minutes to make my presentation. I met him at his Baton Rouge office and presented seventeen storyboard ideas, hoping to sell two or three and get hired. The man got down to business right away. "Hello Mr. Seder, what do you have for me?"

The storyboards were mounted on large foam core boards and placed on an easel. As I described the visuals and read the scripts, Edwards just sat there, mute, poker-faced, disinterested.

His body language confused me. He seemed distracted, yet relaxed and resigned, like a dental patient on nitrous oxide. For most of the fifteen minutes, he stared out the window, avoiding eye contact, expressing no opinion or emotion. "Shit," I thought, "this guy doesn't like anything."

Edwards didn't say a word until I was finished. "Mr. Seder, how much would it cost to produce all those commercials?" High rollers like Edwards don't want to hear answers like, "I'll have to get back to you on that," or "Let me work up a production budget." So I gave him a nice, round six-figure sum and without skipping a beat, he said, "See my brother Marion in the office next door and he'll write you a check." I felt what must have been a significant endorphin secretion that lasted for the rest of the day. I produced twenty-eight commercials during the campaign.

The most complicated ad called for three thousand supporters to assemble on the steps of the Baton Rouge State Capitol while Edwards, standing in front of the group, spoke to the camera. I had asked him to memorize the script.

The spot opened on a close-up of Edwards, then zoomed out and boomed up to reveal the multitudes behind him. A second camera covered the crowd, and a helicopter camera got wide shots. I asked Edwards if he would like to rehearse the script a few times and he declined. "Just roll the camera" he said.

Seconds after shouting "action," I had a very bad feeling. Edwards was not delivering the script I wrote. He was talking about education, jobs, the economy, all the right stuff, but he was improvising! WTF?! I looked over at my production assistant who was timing his delivery, and she said "twenty-eight seconds."

Edwards started to walk off the set. "Did you get what you needed, Mr. Seder?" "Uh, that was very good governor, but could we do just one or two more?" He did one or two more and they were all under thirty-seconds, and flawless. I had never seen anything like this before. Tom Buckholtz, our talented cameraman, looked down at me from his perch on the forty-foot crane and gave me a thumbs up.

When I shouted, "That's a wrap," the band started playing and the crowd headed for the beer and food trucks in the Capitol parking lot. In his biography of Edwards, Leo Honeycutt wrote, "Whoops and hollers gave the ambitious television commercial another spark of energy. Such energy combined with Edwin's onslaught in the media and on the stump gave him a solid fifteen-point lead by mid-summer."

At 6:00 a.m. the next morning, my crew met once again on the steps of the State Capitol. There was no cast of thousands, only two men in white uniforms struggling to carry an old upright piano up the steps of the Capitol building. One of the guys (Dave Treen) loses his grip several times. Here are the script and still frames:

"Piano" 30-sec. TV

(VO) Dave Treen has lost his grip.

He let a five hundred million dollar surplus

slip through his hands.

He mishandled the budget,

giving us the largest deficit in Louisiana history.

He dropped millions of dollars in funding for education,

senior citizens and small businesses.

He tripped over his own revenue projections

which were off by nearly have a billion dollars.

And now, he's trying to hold on for another four years.

Dave Treen has lost his grip.

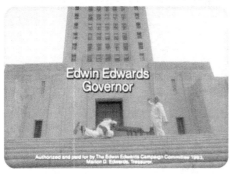

(Sound effect of piano falling to ground)

A series of 10-second ads featured scenes from the original 1953 movie, *Titanic,* shot in black and white. Here is one of the scripts:

"Titanic" 10-sec. TV

(FX: ship's horn)

(VO) With Captain Dave Treen at the helm,

Louisiana suffered the largest deficit in the state's history.

The denouement of our continuing TV drama was "The Final Curtain," a parting shot of satire and ridicule to end the campaign. I had a professional singer record the open and close of Frank Sinatra's "My Way" and used it to bookend a 30-second ad:

"Final Curtain" 30-sec. TV

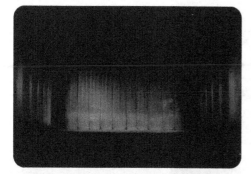

(Music and vocal) And now, the end is near and so I face the final curtain.

(VO) Dave Treen spent a five hundred million dollar surplus,

miscalculated revenues by more than half a billion dollars

and gave us the largest deficit in Louisiana history.

(Music and vocal) And more, much more than this

I did it my way.

Edwin Edwards is a complex man, and it's not within the scope or purpose of this book to attempt an analysis. But I had a blast working on his campaign, which he won with sixty-two percent of the vote.

Two months after the election, Edwards chartered two 747s and invited his friends, supporters, reporters and the entire Louisiana legislature to join him on a trip to Paris (at $10,000 a person to help pay off his campaign debt.) The *New York Times* wrote, "Governor-elect Edwards is not shy about raising and spending campaign money...and so it fell to him to organize one of the most expensive, lavish and bold fund-raising events ever. And to do it in Paris."

In addition to visits with Mayor Jacques Chirac of Paris and President Francois Mitterrand, the schedule included dinners at Maxim's, Tour d'Argent, Le Train Bleu, Le Doyen, a stop at the casino in Monte Carlo, and a formal state dinner at the Palace of Versailles. *Laissez les bon temps rouler!*

6

REPUBLIXAN

This press release was sent out on September 30, 2016, six weeks before the presidential election:

Anti-Trump TV Ad Claims Women Need to Drug Themselves in Order to Vote for Donald Trump

For Immediate Release Sept. 30, 2016
Washington, D.C.

An anti-Trump Super PAC plans to air a 30-second TV ad called "Republixan" in selected battleground states. The ad was broadcast on CNN and Fox News during the Republican convention. (www.yakety-yakpac.com)

Yakety-Yak PAC, a newly-formed, Washington, DC-based Super PAC that produced the ad, is targeting Republican women.

The ad is a parody of pharmaceutical commercials and urges Republican women to talk with their doctor about taking a drug called Republixan – "a little red pill that relieves the stress, guilt and shame associated with voting for Donald Trump."

According to the PAC's director, Deno Seder, "No rational, thinking woman would vote for Donald Trump unless she was drugged."

The ad's producer, Jeorge Seder, remarked, "This is a great ad, believe me, a great ad. An incredible ad. We're going to win so many voters, we're gonna get tired of winning, believe me. It'll make Trump start bleeding from his whatever."

In the ad, a narrator warns of harmful side effects such as "tax cuts for the rich; reduced benefits for women, veterans and minorities; cuts in Medicare and Medicaid; cuts in funding for education; a possible war with Iran and other side effects hazardous to the health of our nation."

This ad and other anti-Trump ads can be seen at www.yakety-yakpac.com.

Yakety-Yak PAC
info@yakety-yakpac.com
www.yakety-yakpac.com

We produced two ads, Republixan and Apple, targeting moderate Republican and Independent women voters in selected swing states who were ambivalent about voting for Donald Trump. During the 2016 presidential election, polls (Gallup, CBS/NYT, ABC/Washington Post, AP/GfK and others) revealed that as many as 74% of women had negative opinions of Donald Trump. Among Republican women, about half said they had negative opinions about Trump. Our ads combined satire with high production values to convey an important message.

"Republixan" was broadcast during the Republican National Convention in Cleveland from July 18 to 21. The ad aired 108 times on CNN and Fox News, including 48 prime time slots during the four-day convention.

Once the ads started running, my phone started ringing. It was the Fifth Estate giving me the third degree. "Who are you?" "What do you hope to accomplish?" "Who's paying you?" "Is Yakety-Yak a real PAC?" And a few other anonymous callers with colorful comments such as, "You mother-fucking piece of shit!"

Here are the script and still frames from "Republixan":

"Republixan" 30-sec. TV

(VO #1) Anxious about voting for president?

Worried about the hateful speech?

Nervous about the treatment of women and minorities?

Talk to your doctor about Republixan,

the little red pill that relieves the stress, guilt and shame associated with voting for Donald Trump.

Republixan. It'll make you feel good about voting wrong.

(VO #2) Warning: Side effects may include tax cuts for the rich, reduced benefits for women, veterans and minorities, cuts in Medicare and Medicaid, cuts in funding for education, a possible war with Iran and other side effects hazardous to the health of our nation.

(VO #1) Yakety-Yak PAC is responsible for the content of this message.

Here are the script and still frames for our second ad, "Apple":

"Apple" 30-sec. TV

(Haunting strings)

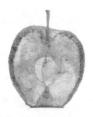

(Time lapse footage of apple rotting. As apple rots, Donald Trump appears in the apple.)

Rotten to the core.

(VO) Yakety-Yak PAC is responsible for the content of this message.

In 1966, California politician Jesse Unruh coined the phrase, "Money is the mother's milk of politics." Our PAC suffered from a severe vitamin D (as in dollar) deficiency from lack of milk. But thanks to friends and family, we raised a few bucks and had some fun.

7

GLADYS AND BERTHA

Like cockroaches, video poker machines are everywhere in Louisiana – casinos, bars, restaurants, truck stops, race tracks. There are more than 13,000 machines in about 1,800 locations, and these ubiquitous five card automatons know how to stack the deck. Video poker collects nearly $600 million in net revenue every year, with $186 million going to local and state governments, supporting such things as higher education, health care, state police, parks and playgrounds.

The *Times-Picayune* called it "the hottest political race in Louisiana in 1996." The voters were going to decide whether or not to abolish video poker. The newspaper also reported that "With a recent poll indicating nearly 70 percent of the state's voters would pull the plug on video poker, the industry is gearing up for a major public awareness campaign." A Baton Rouge pollster told the newspaper that "his poll shows such widespread opposition to video poker that the latest public relations effort is probably a waste of time and money."

John Georges doesn't waste time or money. A successful New Orleans businessman, Georges was the largest video poker operator in the state and was ready to protect his interests. I suggested a straightforward campaign message: If we get rid of video poker and the millions of dollars in revenue, then we either reduce services to our citizens or we raise taxes. So, voters of Louisiana, do you want to keep video poker or do you want to pay higher taxes?

I showed John several TV scripts and got immediate approval to go into production. Here are the script and still frames for "Gladys and Bertha":

"Gladys and Bertha" 30-sec. TV

(Bertha) Gladys, listen to this! Revenue from video poker

produces 180 million dollars for parish

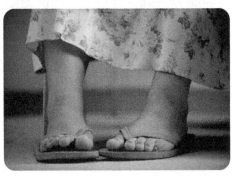

and municipal governments.

(Gladys) Uh-huh.
(Bertha) And the
money goes to raise
teacher salaries,

hire more police, fight
crime and drug
problems…

(Gladys) Mm-hmm.

(Bertha) build roads,
help the handicapped,
provide 15,000 jobs…

(Gladys snores)

(Bertha, annoyed)
GIVE OUT FREE
FACIALS AND
MANICURES!

(Gladys) Free facials
and manicures?

Let me see that. I
don't see nothin' about
free facials!

Gladys and Bertha were big hits, despite a little blowback from a few female friends who scolded me for this slight, albeit unintended, denigration of women. My next ad got even more reaction, this time from the evangelical community, which was, expectedly, opposed to video poker and gambling of any kind. We figured, what the hell, we're not going to get their vote anyway. Here are the script and still frames:

"Preacher" 30-sec. TV

(Preacher) Video poker is evil!

(VO) What's so evil about a game

that contributes 180
million dollars a year
to state and local
government?

(Preacher) Who are
you?

(VO) And 15,000 jobs.

(Preacher) Are you...

(VO) Video poker is
helping give teachers
and police officers a
badly needed pay
raise,

and in ten years, it'll provide two billion dollars in revenue for the people of Louisiana.

(Preacher) That's a miracle!

(VO) That's *money,* and if it doesn't come from video poker, it's going to come from higher taxes.

(Preacher) Taxes are evil!!

(VO) Now you've got it.

Vote YES on video poker. It's a good deal for Louisiana.

(Preacher) Who are you?

The video poker operators spent over $6 million on the campaign, and in the end, held the winning hand. Gladys, Bertha and the preacher helped convince 52.4% of Louisiana voters to keep video poker.

8

WHAT'S YOUR MOTIVE?

It was ugly. The *Boston Globe* wrote, "The battle over a Prevailing Wage Law has eclipsed all other political battles in the state for its intensity and bitterness." The mood in the union hall on that chilly spring morning in 1988 was glum, and the donuts stale. Voters were going to be asked to either repeal or preserve a prevailing wage law – a law governing wages on publicly funded state construction sites, and a law strongly supported by the building trades and opposed by most builders and contractors.

I felt bad for the pollster. As Sophocles opined in *Antigone*, "No man delights in the bearer of bad news." The Boston pollster reported that forty-nine percent of voters favored repeal of the law, while only thirty percent opposed repeal. And many voters associated repeal with tax savings.

Cesar Chavez wrote, "Massachusetts voters had an unusual opportunity to vote on a ballot question that became a referendum on workers rights vs. corporate greed." The opportunity was unusual and so was the campaign. We needed to go on the attack and hit hard against a well-funded opponent, the Associated Builders and Contractors.

If the ABC, as they were called, could repeal the law, they could bring in cheap, unskilled labor from out of state and, according to the ABC, save taxpayer money on state projects. The argument was specious, since the national prevailing law (Davis-Bacon Act) had been temporarily suspended in 1971 by Richard Nixon with disastrous results – sixty-four percent of the contractors actually charged more for construction projects and there were no tax savings whatsoever. Nixon reinstated the act in five weeks. Kentucky also repealed its prevailing wage law and lost 19,000 construction jobs and twenty-seven million dollars in annual tax revenues.

I wrote and produced several ads and videos for our client. Two of them were sixty seconds long and both featured fictitious contractors. My business partner at the time, Lesley Israel, told a reporter, "We had to make them the bad guys and take the tax issue away. We wanted to do something both catchy and substantial." The first ad was called "Liar":

"Liar" 60-sec. TV

(Female anchor at news desk. Building contractor is on screen next to her. He's holding a lit cigar.)

(Contractor) See, if we can just get rid of this law then we can lower your taxes. That's right – lower your taxes.

(Anchor) A handful of builders and contractors want to repeal the Massachusetts prevailing wage law. They say it will lower your taxes. Don't believe it. Since Kentucky repealed its prevailing wage law in 1982 taxes have gone up and the state has lost an average of 19,000 construction jobs and 27 million dollars in state and local revenues each year. Don't let this happen in Massachusetts.

(Contractor) Yeah, but if I can just import some cheap labor from out of state, then I can make more...I mean, then you can save tax dollars. That's it! Save tax dollars!

(Anchor) The Massachusetts prevailing wage law requires contractors who bid on state contracts to pay minimum wages that already prevail. It's a good law and a fair law.

(Contractor) Look, I just want to save you some tax dollars.

(Anchor) Don't be deceived. Question 2 is bad for you. Let's keep the Massachusetts prevailing wage law. Vote NO on Question 2.

Soon after sending the ads to the TV stations, I got calls from two of Boston's three network affiliates, WCVB-TV and WNEV-TV, who refused to run the ads. They said their viewers might not be able to distinguish our satirical ad from their actual news broadcast. So I had to put disclaimers on the ad. I learned later that the WCVB general manager was an ABC man who aired pro-repeal editorials. "The prevailing wage is ripping us off," he remarked in one of his on-air commentaries.

The second ad was a game show, "What's Your Motive?" It featured a host and single contestant – you guessed it, a contractor.

"What's Your Motive" 60-sec. TV

(Quiz show set featuring host and one contestant at desk)

(Host) Welcome to "What's Your Motive?" the quiz show that wants to know, what's in it for you? Today's guest is Byron Cavendish, a wealthy building contractor from Massachusetts. Welcome to "What's Your Motive?" Mr. Cavendish.

(Cavendish) Well thank you Bob.

(Host) I understand that you and the Associated Builders and Contractors want to repeal the Massachusetts prevailing wage law so you can, as you claim, save the taxpayers a lot of money.

(Cavendish) That's right Bob. If I can hire cheap, unskilled labor from out of state to work on public construction projects then the taxpayers gonna get a break.

(Host) But Mr. Cavendish, didn't the federal government try this in 1971 when it repealed the federal prevailing wage law for a short time only to find out that 64 percent of the contractors actually tried to make more money for themselves?

(Cavendish) I'm not familiar with that Bob.

(Host) Come on Mr. Cavendish. This is the show that wants to know what's your motive?

(VO) The motive is profit. Question 2 is bad for your. Let's keep the Massachusetts prevailing wage law. Vote NO on Question 2.

(Cavendish) Bob you just don't understand.

(Cavendish and his desk are pulled off camera)

(Host, waving goodbye) Oh yes we do Mr. Cavendish.

(Audience laugher and applause)

In his book, *Labor at the Ballot Box, The Massachusetts Prevailing Wage Campaign in 1988,* Mark Erlich wrote, "The ads' high production values, their broad humor and their attacks on the contractors eroded the ABC's standing."

At 9:53 p.m. on election night came the first prediction of our victory – 55 to 45 percent for Question 2 (The final vote was 58 to 42). The prediction came from WCVB, the station whose viewers can't tell fake news from real news.

9

HYPOCRITE

William Jennings "Bill" Jefferson was elected as the first black congressman from Louisiana. He served in the army, earned a master's degree from Georgetown and a law degree from Harvard. Our paths crossed several times over the years and I was impressed with his quick mind and political instincts.

In May, 2006, the FBI raided Jefferson's congressional office and his home. They found incriminating evidence in his office and a plastic bag with $90,000 in his home freezer. In June, 2007, a federal grand jury indicted him on sixteen felony charges related to bribery and corruption. He was found guilty on eleven of the charges and sentenced to thirteen years in prison, the longest sentence given to a congressman for bribery or any other crime.

Karen Carter Peterson is a Louisiana State Senator and Chair of the Louisiana Democratic Party. She's smart, articulate and politically savvy. In 2006, a month after Bill Jefferson's office and home were raided, she announced her candidacy for his congressional seat.

We decided to hit Jefferson on the corruption charges, while touting Karen's credentials, platform and vision. Three attack ads were produced featuring an elementary school spelling bee. Six kids were seated on a stage with an adult moderator standing behind a podium. Each contestant approached the microphone and spelled his or her assigned word, while the voice-over narrator maligned the incumbent congressman. Here are the scripts and still frames:

"Corruption" 30-sec. TV

(Girl) c – o – r…

(VO) The FBI says Bill Jefferson extorted money and stock from an African American small businessman.

(Girl) r – u – p…

(VO) Jefferson's wife got $7,500 a month. His five daughters got 31 million shares of stock.

(Girl) t – i…

(VO) Even his brother-in-law and son-in-law cashed in on the deal.

Girl) o – n. Corruption

(VO) And that's just one word to describe Bill Jefferson.

(Boy) Malfeasance. m – a – l…

"Unscrupulous" 30-sec. TV

(Girl) u – n...

(VO) The FBI says Bill Jefferson took over $400,000 in bribes.

(Girl) s – c...

(VO) They videotaped him taking a suitcase full of marked bills.

(Girl) r – u…

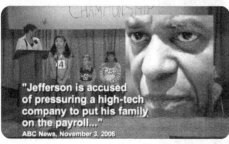

(VO) They found evidence that he extorted money and stocks.

(Girl) p – u – l…

(VO) And now he's under investigation for seven other schemes.

(Girl) o – u – s.
Unscrupulous

And that's just one word to describe Bill Jefferson.

(Boy) Deceitful. d – e – c…

"Hypocrisy" 30-sec. TV

(Boy) h – y...

(VO) Bill Jefferson has been attacking Karen Carter and not telling the truth.

(Boy) p – o...

(VO) Bill Jefferson was videotaped by the FBI taking a $100,000 bribe.

(Boy) c – r...

(VO) $90,000 of which was later found in his freezer.

Boy) i – t – e.
Hypocrite

(VO) And that's just one word to describe Bill Jefferson.

(Girl) Extortion. e – x...

The ads were a smash hit. The satire and ridicule were going to hurt Jefferson. The spots had aired for two days when I got a late night call from Karen's father, Ken Carter. He told me to take the spots off the air. When I asked why, he told me his minister didn't like them. "What does he know about politics?" I asked. "Take them off the air immediately" was his response. So I did. Karen Carter lost the election, 57 to 43.

Of little consolation was the prize won by the "Hypocrisy" ad - Best of Show at the Houston International Film Festival.

10

POTHOLE

There was a pothole in front of my house when I lived in New Orleans. A small pothole. But it grew in depth and width, requiring action by the city, which sent a truck with two men who placed an orange cone in the pothole. Some weeks later, I noticed there were two orange cones in the ever growing pothole. And finally, when the pothole had grown large enough to engulf a compact car, the city erected a three-foot tall orange fence around it. On rare occasions, a crew could be seen filling a pothole – several men standing around the crater while one man shoveled asphalt into it.

In 1983, the New Orleans City Council appointed a Citizens Task Force to explore the feasibility of having the city take over electric and gas operations from the local utility, NOPSI (New Orleans Public Service, Inc.). I was brought in to write and produce a media campaign.

Upon learning that the city wanted to take over the utility, I felt an immediate synaptic impulse in my brain. "Wait a minute," I thought, "the city wants to run a utility when they can't even fix a pothole!" During that aha moment, the spot wrote itself. I called a very talented young cameraman, Kenny Morrison, and told him what I needed:

- A beat-up 1950's vintage pickup truck
- A cast of six men, black and white, including one guy over three hundred pounds
- A dog who could take direction
- A street location with a medium-sized pothole

The spot opens on a 350-pound man sitting on the bumper of a 1949 Dodge pickup truck. The camera pans to reveal three men leaning on shovels while a fourth guy shovels asphalt into a pothole. He is in no hurry to finish the job. A dog lay sleeping near the pothole. The only sounds are the scraping of the shovel and the music, "Up A Lazy River."

"Pothole" 30-sec. TV

(Music) Up A Lazy River

(VO) If you like the way they fix potholes,

you'll love the way
they run the utility
company.

On May 4th, vote
against Proposition 1.

Here's another ad we did for this client:

"Wrestlers" 30-sec. TV

(VO) The citizens of
New Orleans

have taken a lot of abuse.

We've been choked by a 9 cent sales tax.

Slapped with a 7 dollar sanitation fee.

Hit up with a one cent transit tax.

And now we're about
to be clobbered

with a one billion
dollar bill

for the public service
takeover.

We don't have to take
this kind of abuse.

We can fight back.

On May 4th,

Vote against the takeover.

In addition to the TV ads, I wrote and produced a radio ad, "Knockin' " based on the popular 1955 rhythm and blues song "I Hear You Knockin'. " I used a local blues singer and piano player (whose name unfortunately I don't remember) to sing the intro and close lyrics along with an announcer:

"Knockin' " 30-sec. Radio

(Knocking on door)

(Music and vocal) I hear you knockin' but you can't come in.

(Announcer) It's our friends from city hall, knockin' on our door. They want a billion dollars, maybe more.

(Knocking on door)

So when you hear 'em knockin', send 'em walkin' with a message they can't ignore.

(Music and vocal) I hear you knockin'. Go back where you been.

(Announcer) Vote against the billion dollar public service takeover.

The voters of New Orleans decided not to let the city council take over the utility company.

11

1973 BUICK

New Orleans has the highest incarceration rate in the nation. It's double the national average. The Orleans Parish prison was a hell hole – unhealthy and unsafe for the 2,400 prisoners who were locked up there.

For years, drugs and weapons were smuggled into the jail. Prisoners and guards were being attacked. Some were killed. Escapes were commonplace. Conditions were so bad that the prison was placed under a federal consent decree. The feds weren't kidding around. They threatened to take over operations of the jail.

This was the bleak backdrop for Sheriff Marlin Gusman's re-election campaign in 2014. He had several opponents, including the former sheriff, Charles Foti, a 75-year-old cigar chomping no-bullshit kind of politico, who had been first elected in 1973 and served for thirty years.

Ron Nabonne, one of the top political operatives in New Orleans, was hired as the campaign manager. Ron arranged a meeting with me and Gusman. My son, Jeorge and I spent an hour with the man and came away impressed. Gusman has two degrees from Wharton, a law degree from Loyola, is involved in local and national organizations, and most impressive, he has an educated, enlightened view of the criminal justice system and its role in society. He's an advocate for rehabilitation, education and prevention, and revealed an admirable, humanistic attitude toward his prisoners and toward people in general, especially young people. We had a positive first impression, and apparently he did of us since we got the job.

One of our ads focused on the fact that Foti was first elected in 1973, forty-one years in the past. As a visual metaphor, I thought it would be cool to show a 1973 car and talk about Foti being a has-been, a relic of the past, unfit to handle the complexities of today's criminal justice system.

Jeorge prepared a storyboard and we presented it to the sheriff. He loved the idea and gave us a green light.

The Craigslist ad for a 1973 Buick Electra didn't say "mint condition" or "runs well" or anything positive. It did say "needs work." The seller wanted $1,500. He took $1,000 cash.

Since the car did not run, it had to be towed to the studio. The body wasn't in terrible shape, which meant it needed some reverse cosmetic work. My other son, Jonathan, an artist, was given the assignment to "funk it up a little bit." He painted a door primer gray, put some duct tape here and there, did some dental work on the grill with a sledgehammer, taped a piece of black garbage bag where a window had been, ripped off a piece of chrome, smashed a headlight, bent the radio antenna, added a few dents and scratches…and created a work of art.

A bumper sticker on the car read "Vote Foti '73 Sheriff." A Confederate flag decal on the back windshield did not help him with black voters or progressive whites. Here are the script and still frames:

"Buick" 30-sec. TV

(Blues music)

(VO) It's a 1973 Buick.

The same year Charlie Foti was first elected sheriff.

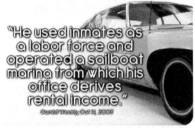

Foti illegally strip searched everyone, even minor traffic offenders.

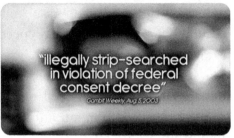

He used inmates to work in a sailboat marina that put money in his pocket.

But worst of all, inmates died from his abuse and neglect,

like the diabetic who was denied insulin,

an untreated inmate

who died of
meningitis,

another from
dehydration,

and others from
beatings and abuse.

Charlie Foti.

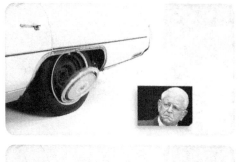

His time has passed,

just like this old Buick.

Re-elect Marlin
Gusman, Sheriff.

Gusman got forty-nine percent of the vote in a multi-candidate field, and won the runoff with sixty-seven percent. After the election, Ron Nabonne wrote, "The spot was a visual attention grabber and broke through the clutter."

I called the guy who sold me the Buick and asked if he'd like it back. He said he did. I let him know that we had done a little body work on the car.

12

BOOZE

Today in America, there is one alcohol-related death every fifty minutes. Nearly thirty percent of all traffic-related deaths involve a drunk driver, and the annual cost of these deaths totals more than $44 billion.

In 1988, Congress wanted to force the alcoholic beverage industry to put warning labels on bottles and cans. I remember attending one of the hearings when a lobbyist from an industry trade association called the Beer Institute presented his arguments against the bill. The DC-based Beer Institute represents the $350 billion beer industry, including over 5,000 brewers as well as importers and industry suppliers.

The lobbyist was creepy and his argument, specious. He brought to mind the children's nursery rhyme from the Mother Goose collection:

I do not like thee, Doctor Fell,
The reason why – I cannot tell;
But this I know, and know full well,
I do not like thee Doctor Fell.

The Alcoholic Beverage Labeling Act passed. It became a federal law requiring the labels of alcoholic beverages to carry a government warning:

Government Warning:
According to the Surgeon General, women should not drink alcoholic beverages during pregnancy because of the

risk of birth defects. Consumption of alcoholic beverages impairs your ability to drive a car or operate machinery, and may cause health problems.

The National Council on Alcoholism asked me to write and produce a national public service radio campaign informing the people about the new warning labels. I wrote a series of ads and included one ad with a little humor, and was pleasantly surprised that it was approved.

"Labels" 30-sec. Radio

(Noisy bar)

(Exuberant announcer) Excuse me, has everyone read the warning label on their alcoholic beverage?

(Crowd in unison) Warning label?

(Announcer) It's right there on your bottles and cans. Drinking alcohol during pregnancy can cause birth defects.

(Male bar patron) Birth defects? I'm not even pregnant!

(Crowd boos)

(Announcer) Sir, is that your bulldozer parked out front?

(Male bar patron) Yeah.

(Announcer) Then read the rest of the warning label. Alcohol impairs your ability to drive a car or operate machinery.

(Male bar patron) So?

(Announcer) So give me the keys. I'm driving the bulldozer.

(Announcer #2) Please, read the warning, heed the warning. A message from the National Council on Alcoholism.

(Sound of bulldozer engine)

I like working on public service and good cause advocacy campaigns. Helps me sleep at night.

13

FOX IN THE HENHOUSE

I told him his quest was quixotic and idiotic. The guy wanted to run against an incumbent Louisiana secretary of state and the son of a popular former governor. "Why don't you just keep chasing ambulances?" I suggested. "There's more money in it and besides, why would you want to move to Baton Rouge?" But New Orleans attorney Doug Schmidt was firm. He was running and he wanted me to handle his media campaign.

Fox McKeithen was elected high school class president in 1964, the same year his father, John McKeithen was elected governor of Louisiana. In 1987, Fox was elected secretary of state. Four years later, Schmidt decided to run against him.

McKeithen had a lackluster first term, which included a few scandals. After reading some of the bad press about him, I suggested a campaign theme: "Fox McKeithen watching over tax dollars is like a fox guarding a henhouse." Schmidt loved it.

Jeorge found a fox costume complete with a huge fox head. He had a suit made to fit over the costume so that only the head, tail and paws showed. I had another shoot out of town, so I told Jeorge he had to direct, produce and edit -- his first time doing everything. He found a chicken farm in rural Maryland, cast an actor to play a farmer with a shotgun chasing the fox, and made a great ad. Tom Kaufman, a talented DC cameraman, shot the spot, which won several national awards for creativity.

"Fox" 30-sec. TV

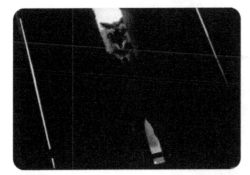

(VO) Fox McKeithen watching over tax dollars

is like a fox guarding a hen house.

The New Orleans *Times-Picayune* wrote,

"Fox McKeithen has abused his power."

The Lake Charles
American Press

called his first term "a
catastrophe."

The Baton Rouge
Morning Advocate

compared the scandals
in his office to those of
Watergate.

And the *Shreveport Journal* said that

"Dismay and distrust...
speaking of McKeithen"
Shreveport Journal

McKeithen's behavior was causing "dismay and distrust" among the voters.

Don't let McKeithen

outfox you.

(dog barking)

Vote for Doug
Schmidt,

Secretary of State.

Schmidt nearly pulled it off. He got 49.8 percent of the vote. The *Louisiana Political Review* wrote, "The master of the deadly funny commercial in Louisiana is Deno Seder, who nearly brought down the secretary of state by having a man wearing a fox head chase some chickens around a henhouse."

14

SOMEBODY LOVES ME

Bobby Jindal was one of the worst governors in modern Louisiana history. He issued an executive order to protect religious business owners who wanted to discriminate against gay customers, he vetoed criminal justice reform legislation, he got sued and lost for preventing low-income people and minorities from voting, he refused to expand Medicaid, he slashed funding for education by more than forty-three percent, and after inheriting a $1 billion budget surplus, he left the state with a $1.6 billion deficit.

Nationally, Jindal will be remembered for his abysmal not-ready-for-prime-time response to President Obama's first speech to Congress. The *New York Times* wrote, "Conservative commentators were among the harshest critics, calling Mr. Jindal's delivery animatronic, his prose 'cheesy' and his message uninspired."

Rachel Maddow told her viewers that Jindal's response "left me literally slack-jawed and babbling like a benadryled infant when I was supposed to respond live on television." NBC News compared him to the Kenneth the page character from "30 Rock."

Slate wrote, "It was a flop that became a go-to lesson on the importance of first impressions in national politics." And conservative columnist David Brooks remarked, "It's a disaster for the Republican Party."

Despite all this, Jindal, who had served one term in Congress, won two terms as governor, our efforts to derail him notwithstanding. Those efforts included a package of 30-second

TV ads produced for the Louisiana Democratic Party. Most political observers assumed Jindal would be re-elected to a second term, so I wrote a script called "Coronation" to satirize the royal crowning. Deborah Thomas, a talented and creative DC theater set designer, built a set reminiscent of some bygone king's court with red and purple velvet curtains, antique vases on pedestals, golden tassels, the works. Two uniformed guards stand in the background and the regal king sits in the foreground. The camera, manned by Glenn Pearcy, an Academy Award nominee, is positioned behind a Jindal-look-alike kneeling before the king, who is about to place a golden crown on Jindal's head.

"Coronation" 30-sec. TV

(Trumpet fanfare)

(King) I crown you governor.

(VO) Excuse me, what are you doing?

(King) I'm crowning Bobby Jindal governor of Louisiana.

(VO) But we haven't even voted yet.

(King) Look, everyone knows Bobby's going to win.

(VO) But everyone doesn't know that Bobby proposed limiting Medicaid patients to five prescriptions per month.

Voted against lowering the cost of prescription drugs.

Supported raising the Medicare eligibility age.

And failed to support
our troops and
veterans by voting
against funding
Tricare, the veterans
healthcare program.

(King) Uh, Bobby let
me hold on to this for
right now.

Bobby Jindal was a bad actor. So bad that he deserved an
award. "Best Actor" features two presenters, a man in a tuxedo
and a woman in a revealing dress.

"Best Actor" 30-sec. TV

(Man) And the final
nominee for best
actor…

(Woman) Bobby Jindal!

(VO) He says he wants good government, but it's just an act.

Jindal took $115,000 from the drug companies,

and $120,000 from the insurance companies.

He was ranked as one of the most ineffective members of Congress

and got a D rating from a nonpartisan Iraq veterans group.

(Man) And the award goes to…

(Woman) Bobby Jindal!!

(Two or three people applaud.)

(They wait for Jindal to come on stage and accept his award.)

(Still waiting)

(Still waiting)

Jindal was a darling of the special interests – drug companies, insurance companies, Halliburton, corrupt foreign companies, cronies of convicted felon Jack Abramoff – you get the picture. As a musical theme for this next ad, I used the 1924 George Gershwin tune, "Somebody Loves Me." For the visual, Jeorge found some old black and white footage of a fifteen foot valentine on a large pedestal surrounded by six 1930s showgirls posing next to the garish prop. The valentine had the words "Somebody Loves Me" written on it. One of the women opened the valentine to reveal a heart with a smiling, smarmy Bobby Jindal in it. The heart and Jindal zoom out as the song and announcer tell the story. Here is the script:

"Somebody Loves Me" 30-sec. TV

(Music and vocal)
Somebody loves me,

I wonder who?

(VO) He talks about ethics,

but took $115,000 from drug companies,

$120,000 from insurance companies,

$7,000 from Halliburton,

and $14,000 from a foreign drug company convicted of Medicare fraud.

(Music and vocal)
Somebody loves me…

(VO) Bobby Jindal, the
best politician money
can buy.

(Music and vocal)
Maybe it's you.

On June 24, 2015, Bobby Jindal announced his candidacy for president of the United States, but couldn't find many people to love him. The man who turned a $1 billion surplus into a $1.6 billion deficit, suspended his campaign on November 17, 2015. *The Atlantic* wrote, "His track record as Louisiana governor did little to help him."

15

GET UP!

There was nothing funny about the 2018 House Republican budget titled, "A Brighter American Future" which would squeeze over $500 billion out of Medicare over the next decade while eviscerating Medicaid by limiting per capital payments or turning it into a block grant program run by the states. Nothing funny at all. And nothing to take lying down, which is why I wrote and produced the following video for a coalition of American hospitals:

"Get Up!" 50-sec. Video

(VO) Sir, what are you doing?

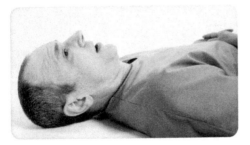

(Man) I'm taking this lying down.

(VO) Taking what lying down?

(Man) The cuts in federal funding for hospital care.

(VO) The cuts in federal funding for hospital care?

(Man) Is there an echo in here?

Over $100 billion dollars
in Medicare and Medicaid cuts to hospitals

(VO) You're taking over a hundred billion dollars in Medicare and Medicaid cuts to hospitals lying down?

(Man) That's right.

(VO) But these cuts could overload emergency rooms, shut down trauma units

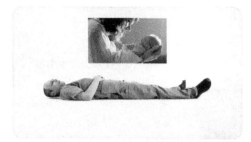

and reduce patient access to the latest treatments.

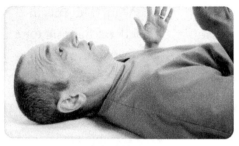

(Man) There's nothing I can do.

(VO) Yes there is! You can get up and go call your senators and representatives and tell them not to cut funding for hospitals

because that threatens patient care and that hurts everyone.

(Man) Really?

(VO) Really. Now get up and go make that call!

1-866-887-CARE
protecthealthcare.org

Coalition to Protect
AMERICA'S
HEALTH CARE

Advocacy advertising is often serious, righteous, and uninspiring. However, a humorous approach to a serious subject can work. On the other hand, if the creative vehicle is not amusing or relevant, it can backfire. I don't advise this approach for funeral homes or right-wing politicians.

16

THEY'RE ANIMALS.
WHO GIVES A SH*T?

The videos were hard to watch – brutal treatment of farm animals on their way to slaughter, pregnant pigs and egg-laying hens crammed into cages so small that the animals could not stand up or turn around, filth and disease all around. Disgusting, cruel and inhumane. Watching these videos was part of my homework before writing and producing a statewide ballot campaign in California.

The 2008 Proposition 2 ballot issue was called the "Prevention of Farm Animal Cruelty Act." Several animal welfare groups supported this initiative, including my client, the Humane Society of the United States, the main sponsor. The initiative required that calves raised for veal, egg-laying hens and pregnant pigs be confined only in ways that allow these animals to lie down, stand up, fully extend their limbs and turn around freely. Our pollster, Bob Meadow, summarized the challenge: "Factory farm interests were dead set against a change in the kind of low-cost, inhumane practices that allowed them to cage and tether animals indiscriminately. The industry raised millions of dollars to defeat this common sense change, and the Humane Society's team had to prepare for an aggressive counter-campaign."

The factory farmers claimed that Prop 2 would jeopardize food safety and public health and drive up prices at grocery stores and restaurants. Bullshit. It was all about profit. These were the bad guys and there could be no justification for their

124

cruel and inhumane business practices. I wrote and produced several ads, two of which featured factory farmers:

"Factory Farmer #1" 30-sec. TV

I'm a factory farmer and I don't like this ballot proposition to stop cruel and inhumane treatment of farm animals.

I mean, who cares? They're animals. We cram chickens in cages where they can't move. So what?

We keep our cows and pigs in small crates. Big deal.

OK, sometimes you have a little problem like that slaughter plant in Chino this year, but look folks, this is not a hotel.

This is business. More
animals, more money.

(VO) Stop animal
cruelty. Vote YES on
Proposition 2.

They're animals. Who
gives a sh... (Cut to
black)

"Two Farmers" 30-sec. TV

(Factory farmer) I'm a
factory farmer.

(Family farmer) I'm a
family farmer.

(Factory farmer) I'm
against this proposition
to stop cruel and
inhumane treatment of
animals.

(Family farmer) I support it.

(Factory farmer) Look, they're animals. Who cares?

(Family farmer) Farm animals should not be crammed into cages so small they can't even turn around or stretch their limbs.

(Factory farmer) C'mon, we're talking pigs, chickens, veal calves.

(Family farmer) That's right, and they deserve humane treatment.

(Factory farmer) They're animals! Who cares?

(Family farmer) I'm voting YES on Prop 2. It'll prevent cruelty and promote food safety, help the family farm and protect the environment.

(VO) Stop animal cruelty.

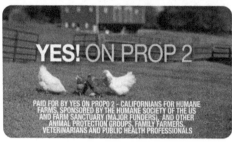

Vote YES on Proposition 2.

Another ad used an entirely different creative vehicle to get the message across to the voters. "Old MacDonald" was challenging because it involved a young girl holding a chicken while singing "Old MacDonald Had A Farm."

The Virginia-based animal wrangler assured me that she had chickens trained to behave on camera. And the little girl we cast assured me she could hold a chicken while singing the song. Well…it required a few more takes than I had planned, but the spot turned out to be the client's and the voters' favorite:

"Old MacDonald" 30-sec. TV

(Girl singing) Old MacDonald had a farm, e-i-e-i-o. And on his farm he had a cow.

(VO) In factory farms, veal calves are chained by the neck and confined in tiny stalls.

And on his farm he had a pig.

(VO) Pigs are forced into metal cages barely larger than their bodies.

With a cluck-cluck here and a cluck-cluck there.

(VO) Chickens are crammed into small cages where they suffer pain and spread disease. You can stop the cruelty.

Vote YES on Proposition 2.

Old MacDonald had a farm, e-i-e-i-o.

We made another ad featuring Ellen DeGeneres, who invited Jeorge and me to join her and Portia de Rossi at a fundraising party in Los Angeles to help get our spots on the air. Several big screens were set up on the tennis courts of some billionaire's mansion in Brentwood. After each spot played, the guests bid on the ads. If they liked the ad, they would bid against each other to see who would put up the most money to air that ad. We raised several million dollars that night.

Proposition 2 made history by winning with 63 percent or 8.2 million votes, more than any other winning proposition on the ballot that year and the most ever for a "yes" campaign in California. Most importantly, farm animals in California are now treated humanely.

17

EVIL TWIN

Our business partner in New Orleans, Karen Carvin, called me late one night, a few days before Thanksgiving in 2014. Did I want to write and produce some radio ads for U. S. Senator Mary Landrieu in her runoff election against a Republican opponent? The Landrieu campaign was not doing well, and reached out to our firm at the eleventh hour.

Mary had served three terms and was the only Democrat holding a statewide office in a solid red state. She was running behind in the polls. Way behind. I felt that whatever we could do, it would be too little too late. And it was. Mary lost her election, but we had fun making her ads:

"The Morning After the Night Before" 60-sec. Radio

(Soap opera music)

(Announcer) And now we return to, "The Morning After the Night Before."

(Gloria, angrily) But Kevin, last night you said…

(Kevin) I know what I said Gloria.

(Gloria) You said we can't afford to lose Mary's clout in Washington because we won't get any more federal money.

(Kevin) Yes but…

(Gloria) You said a freshman in the senate is like your cousin Harold as a tennis partner.

(Kevin) Useless.

(Gloria) You said forget about Democrat and Republican and let's vote for our own best interest...

(Kevin) Honey...

(Gloria) ...and keep Mary because on Appropriations and Energy she brought us billion of dollars to rebuild our homes and passed legislation to revive our economies devastated by the BP spill.

(Kevin) Honey...

(Gloria) Don't honey me Kevin. Last night you were voting to keep Mary's clout and protect our future and now you're thinking about voting for the other guy? The guy who voted against hurricane relief after Isaac! The guy who took money from LSU for work he never did?

(Kevin) But he said Obama..

(Gloria, angrily) (BLEEP) Kevin, we're not voting for Obama, we're voting for Mary – for us, for our kids, for the future!

(Kevin) You're right Gloria. I'm voting for Mary.

(Gloria) And I really do like cousin Harold. He's such a good guy.

(Kevin) Yeah, except for his backhand.

(Announcer) Protect your future. Re-elect Mary Landrieu.

"Evil Twin" 60-sec. Radio

(Announcer) This is the story of Congressman Bill Cassidy and his evil twin, Dr. Bill Cassidy. On the very same days *Congressman* Bill Cassidy was in Washington casting votes and sitting in congressional committee meetings, evil twin *Doctor* Bill Cassidy was in Baton Rouge submitting time sheets for teaching at LSU. When questioned about this fraudulent discrepancy and physical impossibility, Congressman Cassidy said, quote, "I get the same no matter what I do." End of quote. Evil twin *Doctor* Bill Cassidy had no comment. Apparently Cassidy feels he should get PAID tens of thousands of taxpayer funds for a no-show job, all on top of his 174,000 dollar taxpayer-funded congressional salary. On Saturday, send Congressman Bill Cassidy and his evil twin a message. Re-elect Mary Landrieu

In all fairness, Dr. Bill Cassidy did do some good work as a practicing physician in Louisiana. He helped found a health clinic that served low-income families. But that was then, and this was now. Once he got to the Senate, he set his sights on repealing the Affordable Care Act.

Three years after Cassidy's election, Jimmy Kimmel's newborn son had undergone open heart surgery and Kimmel invited Cassidy to appear on his show to talk about insurance for preexisting conditions. Cassidy told him that he would apply the "Jimmy Kimmel test" for any new healthcare legislation and make sure that preexisting conditions were covered.

Four months later, Kimmel tore into Bill Cassidy for the "horrible bill" that he proposed with Lindsey Graham as the Senate tried to repeal Obamacare. Kimmel told his audience and viewers, "He made a total about-face, which means he either doesn't understand his own bill, or he lied to me. It's as simple as that." Cassidy also supported banning annual and lifetime caps for coverage and letting health insurance companies charge different rates for plans based on a person's gender, age and profession.

In August, 2018, the CDC ranked Louisiana the worst state in the nation for healthcare, and most assuredly, Cassidy knew that. Physician, heal thyself.

18

THE MAN

George W. Bush was renominated by the Republican party in 2004. Former Governor Howard Dean was the early Democratic front-runner, but primal screams don't resonate well with voters. Senator John Kerry went on to clinch his party's nomination and chose Senator John Edwards as his running mate.

I had met Kerry when I first came to Washington in 1980, when political media was still a mystery. He invited me and several other Democratic media consultants to his office to talk strategy. I liked the guy. He seemed real and down-to-earth, so when the opportunity came to help him, I did. A friend, Marc Chimes, and I started a PAC – Ipso Facto PAC. This was our first ad:

"The Man" 30-sec. TV

(VO) The man has lead his country in time of war.

He has been strong

and decisive,

fearless

and aggressive.

The man is unwavering in his resolve to fight the battle,

unafraid to attack his opponents,

unashamed to flaunt his power.

The man is our leader

and a great American.

On November 2nd,
vote for the man who
makes the decisions
that affect your life –

the most powerful man
in America.

Re-elect President
Dick Cheney.

Bush won with 53 percent of the electoral votes. The *New York Times* reported that in the three years leading up to his re-election, Cheney got $3.4 million from Halliburton, his former company, plus deferred salary and options to buy Halliburton stock. In 2001, the company won a contract for services in the Middle East for about $5 billion. One of its subsidiaries, Kellogg Brown & Root, got a contract worth $7 billion.

Dick Cheney, "the man," and a great American.

19

CAMEL

I learned two things about camels – they spit a lot and they poop all the time. Not a big, messy poop, but more like Milk Duds. And they aren't actually spitting – it's sort of like throwing up. They bring up the contents of their stomach, mixed with saliva and then kind of spit it out. So if you want to film a camel in a studio, you'll need a raincoat and a push broom. And some peanut butter (more on that later).

Not surprisingly, there were no camels for rent in the Washington, D.C. area. The nearest camel for rent was in New Jersey. Seriously, New Jersey. And it wasn't cheap - $2,000 a day plus expenses. He was a beautiful animal, much larger than expected, and he kept rocking from side to side, as if nervous about going on-camera.

My props person climbed up a stepladder and started piling straw on the camel's back, plus some canteens and canvas bags. The camel didn't seem to mind at all. We shot the beast in front of a green screen so we could add film footage behind him in post-production.

Our dromedary was going to be the star performer in a TV ad about a proposed soft drink tax in Arkansas. The creative hook was based on the idiom, "the straw that broke the camel's back."

We fed the camel some peanut butter to keep his mouth moving and make him more interesting. Here's the script:

"Camel" 30-sec. TV

(VO) Once upon a time,

a foolish king overloaded his camel with many bales of straw.

The king was warned that he was overloading the camel

causing an unwieldy situation.

Not to mention an unhappy camel.

But the king wouldn't listen.

He reached for one last bit of straw

and well, you know the rest.

Like the foolish king, the politicians of Arkansas

have overburdened the taxpayers of Arkansas.

And the soft drink tax is the final straw.

Vote against the soft drink tax.

While we were filming the camel ad, my girlfriend was in Europe organizing an international traveling art exhibition. We had been dating for only a few months, so I thought I would impress her with a little video of me on the camel surrounded by my crew. Two weeks later, she sent me a photo of her riding a camel in Egypt. I knew this relationship was going to work.

Another ad featured my daughter Veronica at age six sitting at a lemonade stand in her front yard:

"Lemonade" 30-sec. TV

(Man) Excuse me, I'm from the government and I'm here to help you.

Uh, that is, I'm here to help you pay your fair share of taxes.

(Girl) Mom!!

(Man) That powdered lemonade mix is subject to sales tax, plus now that you're reselling it,

a soft drink tax that'll help us run the government.

(Girl) Mom!!

(VO) Our government wants us to pay yet another tax, a double tax on soft drinks.

(Man) Two quarts of lemonade at a tax rate of…Are you listening to me?

(VO) Vote against unfair taxes. Vote against the soft drink tax.

In 1992, Arkansas was suffering from a severe recession. Governor Jim Guy Tucker wrote, "The answer was simple: we had to have additional revenue. Someone's taxes had to go up."

From our client's point of view, the bad news was that the tax passed. From Arkansas' point of view, the good news was that the tax revenue was dedicated to the state's Medicaid Trust Fund to help low-income and disabled people.

20

SKEPTIC

They do the most good while I make the least money. But working with nonprofit advocacy clients is gratifying in other ways. Many of the ten million full-time employees in the nonprofit world do noble work in social services, healthcare, equal rights, education, the environment and many other areas. And while these are serious matters in the public interest, I can usually find a way to inject some humor into them.

In Massachusetts, more than 250 farms participate in a program designed to support local agriculture. The nonprofit is called CISA – Community Involved In Sustaining Agriculture, and they wanted me to create a radio campaign promoting their work and their slogan, "Be a local hero, buy locally grown," so I made two ads, "Hero" and "Skeptic." Here they are:

"Hero" 60-sec. Radio

(Street sounds)

(Narrator #1) Excuse me sir, we're doing a survey of consumer attitudes toward locally grown food versus food that's not locally grown.

(Man) OK.

(Narrator #1, sound of paper bag rustling) This is a bag of not-so-fresh produce grown out of state, stored in a warehouse, then shipped over 2,000 miles for consumption here in western Massachusetts.

(Man) Lemme see that.

(Narrator #1, sound of paper bag rustling) While this is a bag of fresh produce grown right here at home by farmers you know and trust. Now, which bag of produce would you buy?

(Man) Is this a trick question?

(Narrator #1) No sir.

(Man) You think I'm an idiot?

(Narrator #1) We think you're an intelligent, well-informed consumer.

(Man) I'd buy dat bag.

(Narrator #1) This bag?

(Man) Dat bag.

(Narrator #1) You picked the locally grown produce.

(Man) What kind of survey is this?

(Narrator #1) An objective survey designed to prove that you're a hero.

(Man) A hero?

(Narrator #1) A hero for supporting local farmers which helps the local economy which helps all of us. Aren't you proud sir?

(Man) I guess so.

(Narrator #1) Excuse me madam, we're doing a survey...

(Narrator #2) Be a local hero. Buy locally grown food and farm products from your neighbors right here at home.

(Farmer) I'm Jim Pitts from Delta Organic Farm in Amherst, and this has been a message from CISA, Community Involved in Sustaining Agriculture.

(Narrator #1, sound of paper bag rustling) And this is a bag of tasteless tomatoes grown thousands of miles away.

"Skeptic" 60-sec. Radio

(Narrator, music) With us today is the world's greatest skeptic, Mr. George Skepticopoulos, who can help you become a local hero by buying locally grown food and farm products. Good morning Mr. Skep...

(Skeptic) What's good about it?

(Narrator) Mr. Skepti...

(Skeptic) George

(Narrator) George, you're a skeptic.

(Skeptic) Maybe, maybe not.

(Narrator) Here in western Massachusetts people want to buy locally grown foods, but like you, they're skeptical. They think it's too hard to find.

(Skeptic) I doubt it.

(Narrator) Doubt what?

(Skeptic) Everything, I'm a skeptic.

(Narrator) So, you think it's easy to find locally grown foods?

(Skeptic) Absolutely. You can find them at your local grocery store, farmers market or farm stand.

(Narrator) Well there you have it folks, no need to be skeptical Right George?

(Skeptic) That's right.

(Narrator) Folks, take it from George Skepticopoulos, the world's greatest skeptic, you *can* find the freshest, best-tasting home-grown food and farm products right here close to home. So be a local hero. Buy locally grown food and farm products.

(Farmer) Hi. I'm J. P. Welch from Justamere Tree Farm in Worthington. And this has been a message from CISA, Community Involved in Sustaining Agriculture.

(Skeptic) Hey, you sure you're a farmer?

J. P. Welch is sure he's a farmer, and his tree farm produces artisanal maple syrup with 100% renewable energy, solar power and locally harvested trees that fuel the evaporator. In 2018, CISA celebrated its 25th anniversary and continues to support local agriculture in Massachusetts every day.

21

TRUTH SERUM

The *New Orleans Advocate* called it "the most expensive and perhaps the nastiest race for a Jefferson Parish district council seat ever seen." My client was spending $2 million of his own money to try and win a job that paid $46,000 a year. As Forest Gump once said, "Well, that just don't make no sense." What did make sense was that the client wanted to pay me to produce two 60-second attack ads.

In 1999, Shane Guidry was a Democrat living in predominantly Republican Jefferson Parish, Louisiana. He lived in an 18,000-square-foot home, complete with a private spa, gym and movie theater. Guidry was an intense, focused, no-bullshit kind of guy from a colorful family. The year before, his father, Bobby Guidry, had pleaded guilty to paying former Governor Edwin Edwards $1.4 million in bribes to get a casino license, and played a key role in getting Edwards convicted of racketeering, extortion, money laundering, mail fraud, wire fraud, Jesus, I'm out of breath. For his help, Bobby Guidry was spared prison time and allowed to keep $80 million he got from selling his casino, the Treasure Chest. I had once asked Bobby Guidry for a donation toward a documentary I was making about a mutual friend, Sheriff Harry Lee. He said he would send me a check when I finished the project, which I did, but never got a check. So if you're reading this Bobby…but I digress.

Shane was running against a fairly popular incumbent, Butch Ward. I told him it would be tough to beat this guy, but he was determined. I figured there must be some ulterior motive, so I didn't delve any deeper. Here are the script and still frames:

"Truth Serum" 60-sec. TV

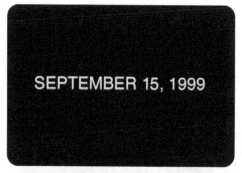

(VO) September 15, 1999.

West Jefferson Hospital.

It was here that Councilman Butch Ward agreed to take sodium pentothal,

commonly known as truth serum,

to dispel rumors that he was unfit to hold public office.

(Ward) That didn't hurt a bit.

(Doctor) Mr. Ward, the truth serum should take effect immediately.

Let's begin with this question.

Have you ever been sued?

(Ward) Ever been sued?

Does a bear sh…
(bleep) in the woods?

(Doctor) I'll ask the questions, Mr. Ward.

(Ward) Man, I've been sued three times by Jefferson Parish for being a slum lord,

and I been sued over a dozen times by people who were hurt on my properties.

(Doctor) What about your nursing homes?

(Ward) Got sued for mistreating some old lady and building a defective nursing home.

(Doctor) Any political deals?

(Ward) Well let's see, a road got built with public funds out in front of my shopping center

which I then sold for a cool 4.7 million.

(Doctor) I see.

(Ward) Hey Doc,

(Ward) I'm starting to hurt all over.

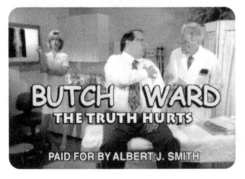

Is that normal?

(VO) Butch Ward. The truth hurts.

Apparently, the truth did not hurt Butch Ward. He won re-election and the bears continued to shit in the woods.

22

POCKET CASH

Senator Herman Talmadge was a real scumbag. The gentleman from Georgia served as a U.S. Senator from 1957 to 1981. A champion of states rights and fierce opponent of civil rights, this reptilian figure was also corrupt. The Senate Ethics Committee, by a vote of 4 to 1, ruled that "there was substantial credible evidence to conclude that possible violations of Senate rules may have occurred and should be investigated." Well, in fact, violations did occur and they were investigated.

Betty Talmadge, the ex-wife, testified to the committee that her husband kept wads of hundred dollar bills in the pockets of an overcoat he kept in the closet of their Washington residence. There were additional pockets sewn inside the coat, so there must have been a lot of cash. She testified that on one occasion she counted about $45,000, and that both she and her husband drew money regularly to pay for their expenses. She told the committee, "It was a way of life for me to live off money from the overcoat pockets. I did it often."

The committee discovered that Talmadge collected $24,000 in reimbursements for official Senate expenses that had never been incurred, plus an estimated $13,000 in reimbursements that were not reimbursable under Senate rules. Talmadge also diverted about $39,000 in campaign funds and other improper Senate reimbursements into a secret Washington bank account he set up in 1973. He called the charges "trivial" and "petty" and blamed his staff for clerical errors. The Senate voted to denounce Talmadge for "reprehensible" official finances and forced him to repay the funds.

In 1980, I got a call from a guy named Mack Mattingly who told me he wanted to run against Talmadge. I jumped at the opportunity to help him. Here is how the *Washington Post* described my new client: "He was an obscure $35,000-a-year IBM typewriter salesman with Indiana roots, fresh-scrubbed and smiley-faced as a Ken doll, and so possessed with confidence and naiveté he actually believed he could dethrone Senate power-broker Herman Talmadge."

Mattingly ran what the *Post* called "a faultless campaign," but polls showed him trailing Talmadge by double digits. The senator had been bragging throughout his campaign that "this has been the most productive session of my career in the United States Senate." I checked his voting record and discovered that during the first eight months of 1980, he had missed more than half of the votes in the Senate. The spot wrote itself:

"Talmadge" 30-sec. TV

(Video of Herman Talmadge) This has been the most productive session of my career in the United States Senate.

(Freeze frame Talmadge.)

(VO announcer) During the first eight months of this year, Herman Talmadge was absent and did not vote on over half of all the votes cast in the United States Senate.

(Talmadge comes to life.) This has been the most productive session of my career in the United States Senate.

(VO announcer) If Herman Talmadge is most productive

when he's absent, let's keep him out.

Herman Talmadge's final and glorious act of televised self-incrimination cost him the election. Mattingly won with fifty-one percent. The *Washington Post* wrote, "The reason this ad is so good is that it actually shows the opponent talking. It works as drama as well as argument." The *Post* gave the ad its 1980 Storck Award for Noteworthy Achievement in the Political Advertising Arts.

23

PANTS ON FIRE

The November 4, 2012 *Washington Post* article headline read, "School board races attract big outside money." I was surprised to learn that one of those school boards was in New Orleans. The article revealed that candidate Sarah Usdin had raised six-figures in donations from people like Netflix founder Reed Hastings, Joel Klein, the former chancellor of New York City public schools, and author Walter Isaacson, former CEO of the Aspen Institute.

The New Orleans public school system had been decimated by Hurricane Katrina. Even before the storm, the system was a mess. In October, 2012, *Huffington Post* reported, "At the time of the storm, the Orleans Parish board oversaw 60,000 students in 100 schools and had become an embarrassing symbol of financial mismanagement and corruption." Seven years after the storm, according to the article, "The city is the national epicenter for innovation in public schooling."

One of the more innovative educators at the time was Sarah Usdin who was running against one-term incumbent Brett Bonin, a Republican attorney. Usdin, a Democrat in a majority Democratic city, was being attacked for taking money from out-of-state, a curious, quaint charge in this political day and age, but effective nonetheless in a town whose politics is still provincial.

Usdin was the real deal – degrees in religion and German, master's in education, Fulbright Scholar, inner city 5th grade teacher, Teacher of the Year, Teach for America's Executive

Director in Louisiana, and a fighter.

Bonin's attacks were hurting, and we had to respond quickly and forcefully. Despite Sarah's laudable fundraising effort, there just wasn't enough money for television, so we decided to run a radio campaign. I wrote and produced some straightforward bio spots and two 60-second attack ads: "Glass House" and "Pants on Fire."

"Glass House" 60-sec. Radio

(Crickets)

(Announcer) It was a quiet night in New Orleans. The town was asleep. Then suddenly…

(Glass crashing, dogs barking)

(Woman) What was that?

(Man) Our crazy neighbor, Brett Bonin.

(Woman) You mean the guy in the glass house?

(Man) Yeah. He's been throwing stones at Sarah Usdin.

(Woman) A guy in a glass house throwing stones? What a hypocrite!

(Glass crashing)

(Announcer) Brett Bonin <u>is</u> a hypocrite. While Sarah Usdin was raising over 60 million dollars for New Orleans Public Schools, Bonin was in Baton Rouge testifying against our public schools getting 300 million dollars already approved by the state. Now he's trying to hide his record by attacking Sarah. Mr. Bonin, people who live in glass houses should not throw stones.

(Glass crashing)

(Sarah) This is Sarah Usdin. I'm not afraid of my opponent's attacks because they're not true. I am a passionate advocate for children and education. I helped start new charter schools after Katrina and raised over 60 million dollars to help our schools, students and teachers. I want to continue to revitalize our school system and bring hope and opportunity to our young people.

(Glass crashing, several dogs barking)

(Man, shouting) Knock it off you idiot!!

(Announcer) Paid for by Sarah Usdin for School Board.

"Pants on Fire" 60-sec. Radio

(Phone ringing, beeps)

(Dispatcher) 9-1-1

(Caller, frantic) I'd like to report a man with his pants on fire!

(Dispatcher) A man with his pants on fire?

(Caller) Is there an echo on the line?

(Dispatcher) Where is this man?

(Caller) Canal and Harrison

(Dispatcher) Are there people standing around him?

(Caller) Yes!

(Dispatcher) Are they shouting, "Liar, liar pants on fire?"

(Caller) Yes!

(Dispatcher) OK that's Brett Bonin.

(Caller) Brett Bonin?

(Dispatcher) He's a candidate for School Board and he's been lying about Sarah Usdin's record.

(Caller) And that's why his pants are on fire?

(Dispatcher) While Sarah Usdin was raising over 60 million dollars for New Orleans Public Schools, Brett Bonin was busy driving to Baton Rouge to lobby against charter schools and charged taxpayers for the gas. Bonin didn't recruit a single program and didn't raise a penny. Sarah helped start 23 charter schools and has dedicated her professional life to education in Louisiana. So to hide <u>his</u> sorry record and lack of experience, Bonin's been lying about Sarah.

(Sarah) This is Sarah Usdin. My opponent has been spreading lies about me. The truth is, I am a lifelong educator, former teacher of the year and a passionate advocate for children and education.

(Caller) His pants are still on fire!!!

(Dispatcher) OK, I'm sending a unit. They'll hose him down.

(Siren)

(Announcer) Paid for by Sarah Usdin for School Board.

The Orleans Parish fire department put out the fire at Canal and Harrison, and Sarah Usdin extinguished Brett Bonin's job on the school board. She won with 58 percent of the vote in a field of three candidates.

24

MISSING PERSON

The dawn light, filtered with a gentle mist, offered the perfect ambiance for filming. I directed Harry Lee, his wife Lai and their twelve-year-old daughter Cynthia to walk casually along the Mississippi River levee as the camera rolled. It was Harry's first TV ad for his campaign for Sheriff of Jefferson Parish, Louisiana, and Cynthia was not thrilled about the cowboy hat I told her dad to wear. Perhaps she wasn't aware of the subtle perceptual and political intent of the iconic Stetson. Thirty years later, it was her turn, but instead of a cowboy hat on her head, I put a gun in her hand.

In 2009, Cynthia Lee-Sheng announced her candidacy for the Jefferson Parish council. She was running in a field of four candidates, including a respected member of the state legislature. Cynthia's credentials were impressive – B.S. in business, M.S. in public administration, CPA, federal officer with the U.S. Department of Justice for over ten years, awards for marksmanship, volleyball coach, wife and mother of two children.

The opposition hit her with accusations of entitlement and estrangement. They said that just because she was Harry's daughter, she didn't deserve elected office. And they said that she had gone to school and worked in Washington for most of her adult life and had lost touch with the people of Jefferson Parish and the issues affecting them. We decided to ignore these charges.

Cynthia didn't like my idea – shooting a pistol at an indoor firing range as part of a TV ad. I convinced her that men would like the image and we needed their votes. I wrote and produced the *de rigueur* TV ads – a bio touting her accomplishments and an issues ad promoting her platform and positions. But that wasn't enough and we knew it. We needed to go after her main opponent, State Senator Julie Quinn.

Our opposition research revealed that Quinn had a few vulnerabilities – she was absent and missed more votes than any other senator on major bills involving taxes, business, health and education; the state ethics board had charged her with campaign finance violations; she was sued by the parish for code violations; and she had been ruled temporarily ineligible to practice law because of some minor technicality. Here's the ad:

"Missing Person" 30-sec. TV

(Police dispatcher VO) Got an APB, missing person, Julie Quinn, state senator.

(VO announcer) Julie Quinn was absent more than any

other senator on major bills involving

taxes, business, health and education.

Absent and getting paid for it with your tax dollars.

She's charged with numerous campaign finance violations

by the ethics board.

Was sued by the parish for code violations.

And was ruled ineligible to practice law.

(Police dispatcher VO) Subject wanted

for violation of public trust.

(Cynthia VO) I'm Cynthia Lee-Sheng

and I approve this message.

And the voters also approved this message. Cynthia beat all three of her opponents and won election to the parish council in the primary, thus avoiding a runoff election.

25

CAN THE POPE SWIM?
ARE FISH CATHOLIC?

They weren't laughing. They weren't smiling. They weren't saying a word. Nothing but silence. I had just made my pitch to the nation's largest association of long-term and post-acute care providers, the American Health Care Association. They hired me to write and produce a video to educate and motivate their 13,500+ member facilities about how to call on their representatives in Congress.

My proposal was to produce a video in two parts – the first would be how <u>not</u> to call on your congressman and the second part would be the correct way to lobby your congressman. By injecting a little humor into the first part, I suggested, the association's members would be entertained and enticed into listening to the second part. But the folks in the room – the folks who provide care and services for millions of frail, elderly and disabled individuals – were stone-faced, except for one guy who finally blurted, "I like it." Then another, then another. Finally, unanimous, albeit delayed approval.

I'm including only the first part of the video, since this book is about humor and satire and there is absolutely nothing funny or amusing in the second part.

"How to Call on Your Congressman" Part I

(Beauty shots of U. S. Capitol)

(VO announcer, music)

This video is about bringing our voice to the halls of Congress. It's for all the people who work in our industry, and it's designed to show you how to have your voice heard in Washington by holding a meeting with your member of Congress. First, the wrong way to conduct a meeting.

(Congressman at his desk. Intercom buzzes.)

(Congressman) Yes?

(Receptionist) Congressman, it's Mr. Brickman from the district's long-term care center.

(Congressman) Send him in please.

(Brickman and congressional aide enter office.)

(Brickman, a comedic actor, with an effusive, overly enthusiastic greeting) Helloooo congressman!

(They shake hands.)

Bill Brickman. Sorry I'm late but it's all your fault. You big poobahs got all the parking spaces. Ha-ha-ha!

(Congressman) Care to take a seat Mr. Brickman. I see you've met my aide, Daniel. You care for some coffee or a soft drink?

(Brinkman) Oh sure. Gimme a double tall cappuccino, low-fat milk.

(Congressman on intercom) Gloria, we need one tall double cappuccino…

(Brickman) Low-fat milk!

(Congressman) Uh, low-fat milk.

(Brickman) Two sugars!

(Congressman) Two sugars.

(Brickman picks up framed family photo from congressman's desk)

(Brickman) Nice looking family. Yours?

(Congressman) Yes it is. What can I do for you Mr. Brickman?

(Brickman) Three things Mr. Congressman. You can lower my taxes, come to my daughter's wedding and tell me who did your weave. Ha! Looks great.

(Congressman) I'm afraid…

(Brickman) Afraid? You have nothing to be afraid of. I have 200 residents, 200 employees and lots and lots of friends all of whom are going to vote for you.

(Congressman) Well that's very kind, but what is the exact nature of your visit here today?

(Brickman) Well I thought you'd never ask, congressman. The exact nature of my visit here today is to tell you that business people like myself need to be committed, I, I mean we are committed to providing quality services for long-term care and that is why we need your support on house bill 123.

(Congressman) Well I certainly want to do everything I can to protect the long-term care financing system, but I'm not sure that bill 123 is the best way to do that.

(Brickman, pulling up his pants, arrogant tone) You're not sure? Ha! Congressman, I represent an 80 billion dollar industry with tens of thousands of voters. You didn't get the memo? Just a little joke. Ha-ha-ha. But all seriousness aside, we need your vote on this one, and as you guys like to say, "Frankly, we think this would be good for the economy."

(Congressman) Mr. Brickman…

(Brickman) Call me Bill.

(Congressman) Bill, this is a tough issue and I don't have all the answers.

(Brickman) Remember, we talked about that at your last fund raiser? The answer is simple congressman. Does the sun rise in the east?

(Congressman) Yes.

(Brickman) Do birds fly in the sky?

(Congressman) Yes.

(Brickman) Does the Pope swim? Are fish Catholic?

(Congressman) What?

(Brickman) Don't you see?

(Congressman, becoming increasingly exasperated) See what?

(Brickman) The answer is <u>yes</u> congressman, and that's what you've got to vote on bill 123!

(Congressman) Mr. Brickman...

(Brickman) Bill.

(Congressman) Bill, do you have anything I can read on this issue?

(Brickman) You don't need paper, just listen to me.

(Congressman) Bill, in a few weeks I'll be gone on a fact finding trip...

(Brickman, singing) After you've gone, and left me cryin'...

(Congressman) Bill, please!

(Brickman points to his Styrofoam coffee cup
on congressman's desk.)

(Brickman) Congressman, are you sure this is low-fat milk?

(Congressman stands up and offers his hand.)

(Congressman) Bill, it's been very nice meeting you.

(Brickman) Congressman, thank you for your time.

(The two men shake hands for about 8 seconds.)

In 2017, Pope Francis told the Italian Swimming Federation, "Through the contact with the water you learn to repulse everything that pollutes, both in sport and in life." So I assume that the Pope can swim, and I'm pretty sure that fish are not Catholic, except maybe a holy mackerel.

26

ORDER IN THE COURT

Louisiana is one of seven states that elect their supreme court justices in partisan elections, one of nine states that hold partisan elections for appellate judges, and one of twenty states that use partisan elections to select their trial court judges. I've worked on a number of judicial races in Louisiana, and most of them tend to be nasty affairs, lacking the decorum of the office to which the candidates aspire. I confess complicity.

Alexis de Tocqueville, during his travels around the country, wrote about the practice of electing judges and predicted that "these innovations will, sooner or later, have disastrous results." More recently, the *Economist* observed, "The spectacle of someone who has the power to hand out death sentences making stump speeches, seeking endorsements and raising funds has long seemed odd to outsiders." And to the insiders, it's assumed that elected judges who get campaign contributions from special interests may have an occasional predisposition to lay a finger on the scales of justice.

The *New York Times* editorial board summed it up this way: "Requiring would-be judges to cozy up to party leaders and raise large sums from special interests eager to influence their decisions seriously damages the efficacy and credibility of the judiciary. It discourages many highly qualified lawyers from aspiring to the bench. Bitter campaigns – replete with nasty attack ads – make it much harder for judges to work together on the bench and much harder for citizens to trust the impartiality of the system." My recipe for attack ads calls for

179

adding a pinch of humor and satire to the stew which can dilute the bitter, nasty taste.

Bernette Johnson, was Chief Justice of the Louisiana Supreme Court, the first African American to serve in that position. In 2018, her daughter decided to follow in her mother's footsteps and run for a civil district court judgeship in New Orleans. Her qualifications were impressive – B.A. in psychology, M.S.W. from Smith and a J.D. from Tulane. She also graduated from the Loyola Institute of Politics, served as a volunteer mentor for young girls, and did a lot of pro bono work in the community.

Rachael was running against two qualified opponents, and things got ugly very early in the campaign. Our opponents were taking pot shots at Rachael, so we decided to hit back, vigorously. One opponent, Marie Williams, had been arrested and booked for violating a court order originating from an accusation of assault. I found her mug shot and used it in a direct mail piece informing the voters of her "criminal" past. The headline under the mug shot read, "You won't see this photo on Marie's Facebook page." The prescient de Tocqueville's was right - "disastrous results" befell our opponent. She told the *New Orleans Advocate*, "That was the lowest, most hurtful thing to me. I couldn't believe they would go that low. They're making me look like I committed murder."

The newspaper wrote, "Fur is flying in the race for a seat on the Civil District Court bench in Orleans Parish, with the release this week of scathing mailers and TV ads from candidate Rachael Johnson." The "scathing" TV ads were directed toward the other opponent, Suzy Montero, the white candidate. With Rachael and Marie splitting the black vote, Suzy was guaranteed a spot in the runoff, or could possibly get fifty percent in the primary and win without a runoff. Rachael was polling in second place. We had no choice but to attack.

We discovered that the IRS had filed a $15,000 tax lien against Suzy Montero in 2011. That's all the dirt we had. Would it be enough? The idea for the TV ads came to me late one night while my band was playing a gig at Clyde's restaurant and bar in Chevy Chase, Maryland. I would get Jerry Perman, our lead singer and guitarist (and prominent D.C. psychiatrist), to sing and record two songs – "Wake Up Little Susie" by the Everly Brothers and "If You Knew Susie" recorded by Eddie Cantor in 1925. Here are the scripts and still frames:

"If You Knew Suzy" 15-sec. TV

(Music and vocal) If you knew Suzy like I know Suzy...

(VO) If you knew that Suzy Montero didn't pay her income tax, would you still vote for her?

Suzy, if you don't pay your taxes, you don't deserve our vote.

(Music and vocal) If you knew Suzy like I know Suzy...

(VO) Rachael Johnson, Judge, Civil District Court

"Wake Up Little Suzy" 15-sec. TV

(Radio static)

(Music and vocal) Wake up little Suzy, wake up!

(VO) Wake up Suzy Montero, because you must be dreaming if you think people will vote for you when they find out you didn't pay your taxes.

Suzy, if you don't pay your taxes, you don't deserve our vote.

(Music and vocal) Wake up little Suzy, wake up!

(VO) Rachael Johnson, Judge, Civil District Court

The ads struck a note of disharmony in the opponent's camp. Suzy told the *New Orleans Advocate*, "I've always paid my taxes. I think the citizens of the United States have the right to challenge whether or not a tax is due. I exercised that right, and the IRS came to a different decision." And so did the voters. Rachael made the runoff and won her election with 54 percent of the vote.

27

OTTO

Congressman Otto Ernest Passman was earnest about civil rights, women's rights, and laws governing congressional conduct. He earnestly opposed all of them. Passman served as a Louisiana congressman for thirty years. In 1956, he was one of the signers of the *Southern Manifesto* voicing objection to the U.S. Supreme Court's desegregation decision in Brown v. Board of Education. In 1974, he was charged with sexual discrimination and lost his case on appeal to the Supreme Court. In 1978, he was indicted for bribery, conspiracy and tax evasion in the Koreagate scandal in which he took a $213,00 bribe from a South Korean businessman, but escaped prosecution because of the statute of limitations. And for several years, he had been cheating the taxpayers by reimbursing himself for expenses he did not incur and which he referred to as "clerical errors." What a piece of work this man was.

In spite of all this, Passman was the front runner in his 1978 re-election campaign. My candidate was Jerry Huckaby, a dairy farmer from a small town in northeast Louisiana. We decided to focus on the cheating issue, since that was something most voters could relate to, and besides, most voters in the fifth congressional district of Louisiana back then probably agreed with Passman on segregation and didn't give a hoot about sexual discrimination or "business deals" with foreign businessmen. Here is how political writer John Maginnis described the cheating issue:

"Passman had been flying home to his district from

Washington, but was filing for driving reimbursement at 20 cents a mile. Over time, the difference between his mileage checks and the cost of the airplane tickets was over $3,000, which Passman pocketed."

So it wasn't the amount of money, but the fact that he lied and cheated. I called a friend who had a 1949 Mercury and we made a commercial:

"Your Cheatin' Heart" 30-sec. TV

(Wide angle shot from back seat of 1949 Mercury. Driver is wearing a Rolex and holding a cigar in his hand. "Your Cheatin' Heart" is playing on the car radio.)

(VO announcer) The taxpayers of the fifth district paid Otto Passman over 5,000 dollars to drive back and forth from Washington, eleven times in six months. The truth is, he took a plane each time, which cost him only 2,000 dollars. Otto was exposed and paid us back. Perhaps it was an honest mistake – eleven honest mistakes. Otto took us for a ride and Jerry Huckaby doesn't like paying for the gas.

Congressman Otto Ernest Passman lost his re-election campaign. His congressional papers can be found in the archives of the University of Louisiana at Monroe, minus any material related to indictments, sexual discrimination or travel expenses. Must have been a "clerical error."

Huckaby beat Passman in the Democratic primary but now faced a new challenger in the general election – Republican Frank Spooner, a wealthy oil and gas producer who was being supported by the national Republican party. Spooner was much more conservative than Democrat Huckaby and he drew national attention. Governors Ronald Reagan of California and John Connally, Jr. of Texas came to the district. Reagan even made TV ads for Spooner, who quickly took the lead in the polls.

The RNC sent a team of consultants to the district to help Spooner. When I heard that, I immediately called my friend and client, State Senator Virginia Shehee, who owned a funeral home in Shreveport, Louisiana. Shehee was the first woman elected to the Louisiana State Senate, and her slogan was, "A woman's place is in the house...and the senate." I asked Virginia if I could borrow one of her black limos for an ad against Spooner. When she heard the script, she laughed and told me to come get the limo.

I hired a great cinematographer from New York, David Seawell, who shot the ad on 35mm film. Sky Hiers, my talented business partner at the time, made the Spooner bumper stickers and the D.C. plates. Unfortunately, a copy of the ad or the script were not to be found. But I did find this description in the *Louisiana Political Review*:

> "Seder put two characters [actually four] in seedy black suits in a Cadillac limousine with D.C. plates and Spooner bumper stickers.
>
> "With the limo driving through cotton fields and kicking up dust, the voice-over says, 'The boys from Washington are telling you how to vote. Let's send the boys home.'
>
> "For added fun, Seder had the car driven around Monroe for a few days. When the commercial aired, many folks said they knew it was true because they had seen the car driving around town."

After living in Louisiana for sixteen years, I learned that most folks didn't like outsiders telling them how to think or act or vote. In fact, it seemed to me, a transplant from Pittsburgh,

PA, that most folks didn't like outsiders period, especially people from Washington, D.C. I used that xenophobia to good effect for Jerry Huckaby. He pulled off an amazing upset with fifty-three percent of the vote.

28

TRUTH IN POLITICS

Mayor Sidney Barthelemy was in trouble. After one term as mayor of New Orleans, his popularity was declining. Sidney wasn't your typical politician. He was soft-spoken, thoughtful, and deferential – qualities I liked about him, but qualities that don't necessarily help you in the polls.

Barthelemy's opponent, Donald Mintz, a lawyer and civic activist, was poised to upset the incumbent. He was presenting himself as smarter and stronger and the voters were buying it. Mintz was respected in the community, especially in the white community. He had been chairman of the Dock Board, the Downtown Development District, the United Way, Touro Synagogue, the Jewish Federation of Greater New Orleans and the Anti-Defamation League. He also sat on the boards of the Chamber of Commerce and the New Orleans Symphony.

But in spite of all these wonderful civic credentials, Donald Mintz was a terrible game show contestant. I sent a photo of Mintz to several casting agencies in Washington and New York. I found a guy in Brooklyn that looked like Mintz' twin separated at birth.

"Truth in Politics" 60-sec. TV

(TV game show set. Big sign with flashing lights – "Truth in Politics")

(Host and one contestant, seated behind desk)

(Music, applause)

(Host) Welcome to "Truth in Politics, the game show that wants to know, is there truth in politics? Today's guest is Donald Mintz, a candidate for mayor of New Orleans.

(Applause, Mintz smiles and waves to audience)

Welcome to "Truth in Politics" Mr. Mintz.

(Mintz) Well thank you Bob.

(Host) Mr. Mintz, you claim to be a tough, capable leader but do you have any experience in government?

(Mintz) Bob, as a tough, capable leader...

(Host) The truth, Mr. Mintz.

(Mintz) Well, no, but...

(Host) Next question. Do you have any experience with patronage?

(Mintz) No sir!

(Buzzer)

(Host) Not true, Mr. Meese. [Edwin Meese had been Ronald Reagan's Attorney General]

(Mintz) Uh, that's Mintz.

(Host) You received millions of dollars in legal fees during the Morial administration.

(Mintz) But listen…

(Host) You say you oppose taxes.

(Mintz) Yes.

(Host) Have you ever proposed a new tax?

(Mintz holds hand in air.)

(Mintz) Never.

(Buzzer)

(Host) The truth is, Mr. Mintz, you were the leading supporter of the earnings tax.

(Mintz) Bob, please…

(Host) You claim to be able to bring jobs and business to New Orleans.

(Mintz) Mm-hm.

(Host) But when you were president of the Downtown Development District we lost businesses and jobs all up and down Canal Street. Isn't that true?

(Mintz) Well I'm not sure…

(Buzzer)

(Host) The truth Mr. Mintz!

(Mintz and his desk are pulled off-camera.)

(Mintz) Bob, you just don't understand!

(Host) Oh yes we do, Mr. Mintz.

(Host waves goodbye to Mintz.)

(Applause)

There were two consequences from this ad, one expected and one completely unexpected. We expected the 60-second game show to hurt Mintz and it did. What we did not expect was that he would accuse us, bizarrely, of anti-Semitism, which was laughable and pathetic. We did not attack him because he was Jewish, we attacked him because he was not telling the truth. Sidney Barthelemy was re-elected with 55 percent of the vote.

29

WHERE'S MY PIE?

After serving three terms in the Kansas House of Representatives, Kathleen Sebelius announced her candidacy for Kansas Insurance Commissioner in 1994. To her credit, she refused to take campaign contributions from the insurance industry and was the first candidate for any office in Kansas to make that pledge. I was told that she was also the first candidate to inject a little humor in her campaign.

Sebelius stunned the political experts by beating her Republican incumbent – the first time a Democrat had won that office in more than ten years. She became the only Democrat to hold statewide office in Kansas. Four years later, she ran for re-election. This my favorite TV ad of her campaign:

"Where's My Pie?" 30-sec. TV

(Doris) And a piece of pie.

(Martha) Doris, have you heard what they're saying about Kathleen Sebelius?

(Doris) No, what?

(Martha) "Kathleen Sebelius stands for the people in a way few politicians do."

(Doris) That's nice.

(Martha) "Sebelius has brought a higher level of respectability to the office."

(Doris) Uh-huh.

(Martha) "Sebelius does not take money from the insurance industry."

(Martha VO) "She works for us, not for them."

(Martha) "Kansas has a gem in the Insurance Commissioner's office and we should keep her there."

(Doris) That's great. But where's my pie?!

(VO) Kathleen Sebelius. Your Insurance Commissioner.

Sebelius went on to serve two terms as governor and was appointed Secretary of Health and Human Services by President Obama. I assume Doris eventually got her pie.

30

DEAD FISH

He was the first politician in Louisiana and the second in United States history to have been elected as both speaker of his state house of representatives and president of his state senate. John Joseph Hainkel, Jr. was known as a raconteur and good ol' boy who switched parties and became a conservative Republican. The *Times-Picayune* wrote of him, "He moved at ease between the world of gentility and the tobacco-chewing country store crowd. He frequently wore madras clothes with mismatched shirts, whether he was in the halls of power or at his St. Francis of Assisi Catholic Church parish."

The caller never told me why he wanted Hainkel defeated, and I didn't ask. Two scripts were approved, the money was wired, and TV commercials were sent (including another game show!) Oh, if only they were all this easy.

I wrote a script which was a parody of a popular PBS show about books and asked Dick Bangham, a very talented local graphic designer, to come up with a book jacket with the title, "Sleazeball, The Story of Senator John Hainkel," including a big, unflattering photo of the sleaze...I mean, senator.

"Sleazeball" 30-sec. TV

(Bradford) Hello. I'm Don Bradford, your host for "Book World."

And this is our book of the week –

"Sleazeball, The Story of Senator John Hainkel."

Read how Hainkel got thousands of taxpayer dollars for members of his family.

How he cut a deal
with a state agency
and made over 6
million dollars.

How he changed a law
so he could sue the
state and make over 9
million dollars.

"Sleazeball, The Story
of Senator John
Hainkel" –

a fascinating story of
greed and corruption.

For the second ad, I had Bangham design a big sign for a game show – "What's That Smell?" In addition to the show's name, it featured a huge, bulbous cartoon nose. Set designer extraordinaire, Deborah Thomas, came up with a wonderfully tacky game show set. Two of my favorite local actors, Paul Anthony and Michael Willis, played the host and blindfolded contestant, respectively.

"What's That Smell?" 60-sec. TV

(Music, applause)

(Host) Welcome to "What's That Smell?" Our next contestant is Gary Willis from Metairie, Louisiana.

Ready Gary?

(Gary) Ready Paul.

(Host) Gary, you need four correct answers to win the grand prize. So tell us if you can, what's that smell?

(Gary) Limburger cheese

(Bell)

(Gary) Sneakers

(Bell)

(Host) Go Gary!

(Gary) Oh man, dead fish

(Bell)

(Host) You need one more Gary!

(Gary) Um, pass, pass!

(Host) Next item

(Gary) Whoa, that's nasty!!

(Host) What's that smell Gary?

(Gary) O-o-o-o that really stinks!

(Host) What is it Gary?

(Gary) That's gotta be...

(Gary) That's gotta be Senator John Hainkel's record!

(Bell)

(Host, hysterical) Senator John Hainkel's record!

Congratulations Gary!! Our new winner!!

(VO) John Hainkel funneled thousands of taxpayer dollars

to members of his family.

He cut a deal with a state agency

and collected over six million taxpayer dollars in legal fees.

He got a law changed

so he could sue the state of Louisiana and

collect over nine million taxpayer dollars in legal fees.

John Hainkel's record.

It really does stink.

John Hainkel won re-election and today, the only smell reminiscent of this Louisiana lawmaker is the smell of marble in the rotunda of the Louisiana State Capitol where a bust of John Hainkel was placed in 2006, a year after his death.

31

FLOATING HAMBURGERS

It just didn't make any sense. "A businessman for the business of education." What the hell did business have to do with education? Unless maybe you were a business major. Louisiana Superintendent of Education Louis Michot thought he could coast into a second term with that inane slogan. I guess the college dropout figured if he could successfully manage forty-five Burger Chef restaurants, he could manage 1,400 public schools. Talk about a non sequitur!

Michot and his predecessor, Bill Dodd, presided over an education system that ranked 49th in the nation on virtually every measure of educational achievement. In adult literacy, the state ranked last in the nation.

At least Bill Dodd had been a schoolteacher, but as Superintendent of Education, he was hampered by the full implementation of desegregation in Louisiana public schools ordered by the federal courts and not by his office.

Enter Kelly Nix, a professional educator with a master's in education, plus additional graduate studies and teaching experience at the college level where he taught public administration. Nix had also worked as a researcher for the Public Affairs Research Council, a good government type of advocacy organization. I wrote several ads promoting Nix's qualifications and vision for improving education in the state. But that wasn't enough. Our polls showed Nix gaining on Michot, but not fast enough to overtake him by election day. We needed to go on the attack. We needed to give him the business.

"Hamburgers" 30-sec. TV

(Music: Blue Danube Waltz)

(VO) You're looking at Louis Michot's main qualification for superintendent of education–

his 10 million dollar hamburger business.

It must take up a lot of his time,

like the time he spent running for political office –

5 times in the past 12 years.

We don't need a businessman or a politician.

We need a full-time educator.

Hold the onions, Mr. Michot.

We need businessmen for business, educators for education.

Kelly Nix, superintendent of education.

The waltzing hamburgers were a big hit. Political writer John Maginnis wrote, "Soon viewers were laughing at this strange commercial with cartoon hamburgers floating to the music of 'The Blue Danube.' " We hit Michot with another ad, "ABC" in which we lumped him in with his predecessor, Bill Dodd.

"ABC" 30-sec. TV

(VO) Every wonder what happens to a political promise?

You're looking at one.

It was a promise made
by Bill Dodd and
Louis Michot.

They promised us
better education in
Louisiana.

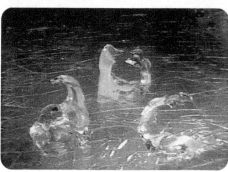

They said wait, be
patient, it'll come.

We've waited 12 years.
It never came.

Instead, we're now
ranked last nationwide
in adult literacy.

Last, and still waiting.

Kelly Nix
Superintendent of Education

In 1975, during the ancient analog era, no one was writing and producing humorous or satirical political ads in Louisiana or in the nation for that matter, with one exception – Tony Schwartz, the creative, agoraphobic television genius in New York who inspired me to do the work I do. He taught me that sometimes a good concept doesn't need frenetic editing or special effects to communicate a message. Sometimes a good concept, whether it's floating hamburgers or melting ice sculptures, is all you need.

32

NOT GOOD LARRY

Sheriff Jack Stephens was a big, imposing man at six feet, seven inches, and he was in trouble. While dealing with issues of cronyism and conflicts of interest, Stephens was also facing a tough re-election campaign against a local insurance salesman named Larry Landry, who had his own issues.

The chemistry wasn't right between me and Stephens and I just wanted to do my job and get out of Dodge as quickly as possible.

I don't recall many details about this campaign and don't want to. But I do fondly recall an ad we did for this guy. We cast locally for a comedic actor and found someone who was terrific. There was no budget for a studio, so we filmed in my rental cottage with a small crew. Jeorge and I designed a funky, minimalist set. When the whole crew is laughing during filming, you know you've got something.

"Not Good Larry" 30-sec. TV

LARRY LANDRY'S POLLSTER
(A DRAMATIZATION)

(Pollster) The poll numbers are not good Larry.

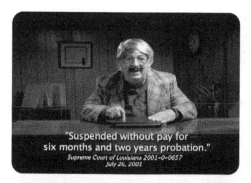

"Suspended without pay for six months and two years probation."
Supreme Court of Louisiana 2001-0-0657
July 26, 2001

The voters don't like that you got suspended and put on probation for two years as justice of the peace.

Landry was sued 4 times in the past 2 years.
34th Judicial District Court for the Parish of St. Bernard
State of Louisiana

They don't like how you got sued over and over as an insurance agent for mishandling claims.

"Maxwell Landry identified as responsible for distribution of cocaine."
U.S. District Court, Eastern Div. of LA
U. S. of America vs Maxwell Landry Aug. 1, 2007

And they're not too happy that your son got busted dealing four pounds of cocaine

"The early morning raid netted 42 Pit Bull Terriers...5 dead dogs."
The Times-Picayune, April 25, 2007

not to mention his dog fighting right next door to your own house that you must have known about.

Not good Larry.

(VO) Larry Landry.

(VO) Not good for St. Bernard.

(Pollster) Not good at all Larry.

The ad got lots of free exposure on local news shows and "Not good Larry" became a popular mantra among local political junkies as well as among my family and friends. Stephens won re-election by 115 votes.

Shortly after the campaign, Jeorge and I were standing in the checkout line at the Whole Foods on Magazine Street. The couple in front of us were having some sort of disagreement. The woman was scolding her husband, "But I told you to get grapes! Not good Larry!" The cashier, shaking her head, added, "Not good at all Larry."

33

1 – 8 0 0 – Y O U – S U C K E R

New Orleans Mayor Marc Morial wanted to change the city charter so he could run for a third consecutive term. His father had tried it fifteen years earlier, but failed. Morial raised and spent over one million dollars trying to convince the voters that he deserved a third term. The opposition strategist, attorney and political operative Ron Nabonne, wrote that "The strategy of the opposition was to ridicule and make fun of the proposal in an effort to counter the overwhelming political and financial support behind Morial's campaign." I wrote and produced two 60-second radio ads in that effort – "1-800-YOU-SUCKER" and "Dead Horse."

"1-800-YOU-SUCKER" 60-sec. Radio

(Announcer #1) I hear you're thinking about voting to change the charter so the mayor can run for a third term. Well check it out. Here's what they want you to believe. If you pass a third term amendment, the mayor runs again, the schools get fixed, everybody's happy. Well if you believe that, call this toll-free number 1-800-YOU-SUCKER and I'll make you a deal on some ocean front property in Kansas. Don't like the water? No problem. We'll turn the Superdome into a condo and I'll sell you one at a very good price. That's 1-800-YOU-SUCKER.

(Announcer #2) Don't believe what you hear about the third term amendment. Don't believe that by changing the charter to let the mayor run for a third term, the schools can be fixed. It's not that simple. The truth is that changing the charter won't do anything but give the mayor another term in office. It won't improve the schools. It won't stop crime. It won't fix potholes. If you buy Proposition A, you'll buy anything.

(Announcer #1) How 'bout an original New Orleans subway car?

(Announcer #2) Don't be a sucker. Vote no on Proposition A. And do not Call that 1-800 number.

(Announcer #1) How 'bout a nice Rolex?

(Announcer #2) Paid for by Citizens to Save Our Charter.

(Announcer #1) Looka here. George Washington's teeth!

(Sound of teeth chattering)

"Dead Horse" 60-sec. Radio

(Music)

(Sound of baseball bat hitting sack of grass seeds)

(Male voice in distance) Get up!!

(Announcer) Our mayor is beating a dead horse.

(Bat hits sack twice.)

(Male voice) I said get up!!

(Announcer) He's trying to revive an idea that died years ago - the idea of changing our home rule charter so that a mayor can run for a third consecutive term. But unfortunately for the mayor...

(Sound of bat hitting sack)

...this horse is dead. In three different past elections, the voters of New Orleans rejected the idea of changing our charter so that a mayor could run for a third consecutive term. It was bad idea then, it's a bad idea now.

But the mayor carries a big stick...

(Sound of bat hitting sack)

...and he just won't stop. The real issue, the only issue is this – should we change our home rule charter to satisfy the political ambitions of any one person? The charter provides a check and balance against the abuse of power, and creates the opportunity for fairness, new people and fresh ideas.

(Sound of bat hitting sack)

The mayor is beating a dead horse. Vote no on Proposition A.

34

LOUIE LOUIE

First, they tried to disqualify my client from running for office on some legal technicality. When that didn't work, both candidates went to court and asked a judge to force their opponents to take their attack ads off the air.

My client, Chris Roberts, was running for another term on the Jefferson Parish, Louisiana Council. One of his two opponents, Louie Congemi, had been the mayor of a small town and was an astute politician. Both men were playing hardball politics. Lawyers for the two men met for several hours to hammer out an agreement before presenting it to the judge. Here is how the *Times-Picayune* described the situation:

> "Jefferson Parish Councilman Chris Roberts and Louis Congemi have settled a dispute over political commercials that claimed Roberts hasn't paid his taxes in five years after Congemi agreed to stop running the ads. In turn, Roberts has agreed to pull a negative ad targeting Congemi that's set to the song 'Louie, Louie.' "

I love the song, "Louie, Louie" by the Kingsmen, and it was perfect for this campaign. Lucky for us, the fair use clause of the copyright law allows using copyrighted material for "a limited and transformative purpose, such as to comment upon, criticize, or parody a copyrighted work." Or in our case, to transform Louie Congemi into a losing candidate.

With Jeorge Seder on guitar backed by his band, me on

keyboard, and D.C. vocalist Tommy Lepson belting out the lyrics, we recorded a 30-second soundtrack for TV and a 60-second track for radio.

Next, our local producer, Tam Kady, found a vintage 1960's jukebox in mint condition, a crew was assembled, and a spot was born:

"Louie, Louie" 30-sec. TV

(Music and vocal)
Louie, Louie, oh yeah,

you gotta go now.

Yeah,

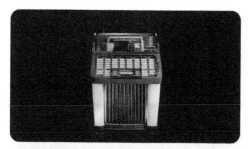

yeah,

yeah,

yeah.

(VO) Louie Congemi, you were cited by the Ethics Board for getting free personal services from a city contractor.

You were investigated

223

by the FBI for illegal campaign activities.

You told a city employee

to lie about her felony conviction.

Louie Congemi,

you gotta go now.

(Music and vocal)
Louie, Louie, oh yeah,

you gotta go now.

And here is the 60-second radio ad:

"Louie, Louie" 60-sec. Radio

(Music and vocal)

Louie, Louie, oh yeah, you gotta go now. Yeah-yeah-yeah-yeah.

(Announcer) Louie Congemi, you gotta go.

You were cited by the Ethics Board for getting free personal services from a city contractor.

You were investigated by the FBI for illegal campaign activities.

You told a city employee to lie about her felony conviction.

Your wife was employed by a public contractor while you were in public office.

You took tens of thousands of dollars in campaign contributions from a Jefferson Parish Section 8 program contractor who was cited in a report by the Inspector General.

And when the *Times-Picayune* asked you to comment on these activities, the paper reported, quote, "He did not return phone calls for comment."

It's time to face the music.

Louie Congemi, you gotta go.

(Music and vocal) Louie, Louie, oh yeah, you gotta go now. Yeah-yeah-yeah-yeah.

(Chris Roberts) Paid for by the Chris Roberts Campaign Fund.

The ads ran for ten days before both candidates agreed to pull their attack ads. But our parody did its damage. A majority of voters agreed that "Louie, Louie, you gotta go now." Chris Roberts got fifty-one percent of the vote, Congemi got twenty-five and a third candidate got twenty-four.

35

PAPER OR PLASTIC?

Carol Leifer is funny. And multi-talented. She's a comedian, writer, producer and actress who appeared as a guest on Late Night with David Letterman twenty-five times, as well as guest appearances on The Tonight Show with Jay Leno, Late Night with Conan O'Brien and many others. She was a writer for Saturday Night Live, Seinfeld, The Larry Sanders Show and the Academy Awards. She's created and produced sitcoms, comedy specials and won four Emmys.

I called her agent and told her that I thought Carol would be perfect as the on-camera star of a video on food labels. My suggestion was met with a long, uncomfortable silence. The agent didn't think Carol would be interested, but she would ask. I explained that it was a public service video about a new law (the 1990 Nutrition Labeling and Education Act) that required all packaged foods to bear nutrition labeling, and any health claims needed to be consistent with terms defined by the Secretary of Health and Human Services. The agent asked me to send the script and promised to get back to me within a week.

Leifer agreed to do the video if we shot in the Los Angeles area. No problem. We found a grocery store (Vons) in Pasadena and scheduled the shoot. The client, Public Voice, was a little nervous about using a comedian to educate the public about a serious topic like nutrition labeling, but I convinced them that by adding entertainment value, we could increase viewership. Here are a few excerpts from the video:

"Smart Selections for Healthy Eating" 6-min. Video

(Intro titles, music)

(VO announcer) Public Voice presents "Smart Selections for Healthy Eating," a video guide for using the new food labels featuring comedian Carol Leifer .

(Scenes of Carol Leifer pushing cart in grocery store)

(Carol) Hi. I'm Carol Leifer and thanks for watching this video. You are truly a concerned consumer, and these days, you <u>should</u> be concerned. Good nutrition has become a lot more complicated. You know, to me, the four food groups used to be Twinkies, Ding Dongs, Gummy Bears and Ho Hos. Nowadays, trying to make smart selections is much more difficult. Consumers really needed new labels on foods to give them health and nutritional information, but before we go any further, I know what you're thinking, you're saying Carol Leifer, she's a comedian, so where's the joke? Have you read the labels on some of the foods you buy? I mean there's the joke.

(Carol takes a food product off a shelf.) Look at this.

(Carol reads from the product package.) More fiber. More fiber than what? Carpet remnants? Everything on the shelf seems to be screaming at you–I'm lite this. I'm healthy that. Low, high, reduced, fortified. Hey, I'm hungry over here! I need some serious information.

(Carol takes package from shelf.) The front of the package is what gets your attention and makes you want to buy the product. Until now, it's been pretty loose. For instance, a label might have said that a product was lite, without telling you that it was only light in the box.

(Carol shakes box.)

(Man is seen pushing cart in aisle behind her. Staring into space, zombie-like, he is saying "Low fat, less sodium, all natural, more nutritious…")

(Carol watches him pass by.) Yes folks, you just saw it right here. It's supermarket of the damned!

(Carol explains the components and benefits of the new labels.) During 1993, more and more products will be featuring the new labels, which don't become mandatory until the middle of 1994, so you can stop eating until then or, if you want the benefits of the new labels, you may want to look for them on the foods you buy.

(Carol looking into frozen ice cream freezer. She turns to camera and pats her nose.) Oh, my nostrils are frozen. Reminds me of an ice cream you might find here in the frozen food section – Frozen Schnozen.

(Carol as cashier at checkout counter) Thank you for taking the time to watch this video. Those of you who would like to stay for an extensive quiz on the material you've just seen, feel free. All others, I hope you've seen the benefits of reading food labels carefully and making smart selections. If not, I hope this was a painless way to kill a few minutes.

I'm Carol Leifer for Public Voice.

(Carol turns to customer.) Will that be paper or plastic sir?

36

EDWIN'S BROTHER

The Louisiana Fifth Circuit Court of Appeal has jurisdiction in five parishes. My client and friend, Marion Edwards, was eminently qualified for that position. He had years of legal experience and was a judge and former prosecutor. He was respected in his community (Gretna) and had the right temperament for a judge, but had one unfortunate disadvantage – he had the same name as the brother of former Governor Edwin Edwards, and that was causing some confusion among the voters.

Edwin Edwards had served four terms as governor. His last term ended in 1996, two years before my client announced his candidacy for the court of appeal. I knew the governor's brother, having worked with him during two of the governor's campaigns. He was a sharp lawyer, an astute campaign manager, and a ferocious fundraiser. He also had a great sense of humor. But he was not a candidate for judge. Pollster Joe Walker told us that he had a thirty-nine percent negative rating

People were asking, "Why is the governor's brother running for judge in the fifth circuit? He lives in Baton Rouge!" Others were dredging up less than flattering things about the brother, such as the federal charges for racketeering, conspiracy and corruption (eventually dropped). An Associated Press report said that "Prosecutors referred to Marion as a 'bag man' for Edwin. Marion later lampooned that characterization by walking into a French Quarter bar with a shopping bag on his head." None of this was helping Marion Edwards, the candidate for judge.

The creative and strategic challenge was to differentiate Marion the candidate from Marion the brother while touting the candidate's experience and qualifications. Here is how we did it:

"No I'm Not" 30-sec. TV

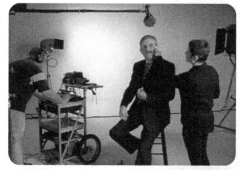

(Director VO) Rehearsal!

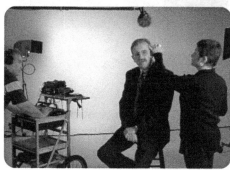

(Marion) I'm Marion Edwards, Judge of Division O

and candidate for the court of appeal. I was also a prosecutor in Jefferson Parish for 25 years.

(Sound man) You Edwin's brother.

(Marion) No I'm not.

I put people in jail who need to be there.

On my own time, I preside over a special drug court

that forces first offenders to remain drug free,

keep jobs, pay their own way and become productive members of society.

If that's the kind of judge you want,

please vote for me.

(Gaffer) You Edwin's brother.

(Marion) No I'm not.

(VO) Judge Marion Edwards, Court of Appeal.

We convinced enough voters that Marion Edwards was not his namesake. He won the election and served on the court for fourteen years. When Marion Edwards, the brother, died in 2013, the *Times-Picayune* ran a picture of Marion Edwards, the judge, who called his friends to quote Mark Twain, "The report of my death was an exaggeration."

37

HOW DO I DISLIKE THEE?

It was the first verdict of "not guilty by reason of insanity" in Louisiana history. Following the murder trial, *State of Louisiana v Peter Paul Bousquet,* the defense attorney, Anthony "Tony" Guarisco, got a lot of publicity. After all, he made history, and what would he do with his new-found fame? The following year, 1975, he decided to run for the Louisiana State Senate.

Tony was an interesting guy. He was an Italian-American duel citizen from a large family in Morgan City, Louisiana. The family was in the shrimp business, the oil business, real estate, and of course, law. Tony was a natural-born leader. While in law school, he had been president of the Student Bar Association and Chief Justice of the Judicial Court of Honor. In addition to his law degree, he had a degree in business and later, earned a master's in liberal arts.

One of his opponents was a popular state representative, Elward Brady, Jr. I wanted to associate Brady with all the things that people did not like about their state government. Inspired by Elizabeth Barrett Browning's sonnet, "How Do I Love Thee?" I created this TV ad for Tony:

"How Do I Dislike Thee?" 30-sec. TV

(Scenes of man in patriot costume and three-pointed hat speaking from balcony of old art deco theater)

(Patriot) How do I dislike thee? Let me count the ways. I

235

dislike thee for fixing the prices on my milk. I dislike thee for raising my taxes. I dislike thee for giving me the worst educational system in the nation. I dislike thee for...

(VO announcer over patriot) The Louisiana legislature. Anthony Guarisco doesn't like what's going on there. Do you?

(Patriot) I dislike thee for the bad roads and highways throughout our state.

(VO announcer) Anthony Guarisco, senator.

Guarisco won his election and served in the legislature for twelve years. I was impressed with his performance, including his compassion and farsightedness. For example, in 1978 he successfully sponsored a bill to permit physicians in Louisiana to prescribe marijuana for people with glaucoma or people undergoing chemotherapy. The Marijuana Control Board was created to monitor the law, but was abolished by Governor Buddy Roemer.

38

LEAN TO THE RIGHT

In 1992, my client, Tom Hecht was a young, progressive Democratic candidate for Congress running in Wisconsin's second district, which included Madison. His opponent was a local TV newsman, conservative Republican Scott Klug. While Madison was progressive, much of the rest of the district and state was not. Pollster Alan Secrest reported that our candidate had one-third of the vote, the opponent had one-third, and one third was undecided.

Hecht was a politically astute candidate. He held a bachelor's in political science from the University of Wisconsin, and a master's in political science from the London School of Economics. He had worked in Washington for Wisconsin Senator William Proxmire, and had a good grasp of political issues.

Tom was a marathon runner so we made a TV ad showing him running while his voice-over talked about the issues. A second ad took a shot at Klug for being too far to the right. The ad looked simple but required a bit of engineering. An eight-foot tall platform was built with a steel pendulum underneath. A rod ran through the stage and up the pant leg of an actor. The rod was fastened to him with a strap around his waste. Two men under the platform operated the pendulum so that the actor could be shown leaning to the right as he addressed an audience of twenty-one people arranged in three tiered rows. Jeorge Seder directed.

"Lean to the Right" 30-sec. TV

(Candidate) As your next congressman, I promise to…

(VO) Have you noticed that Scott Klug

has been leaning more and more to the right?

He's voted against reproductive choice for women,

against cleaning up toxic waste,

against public education,

against senior citizens and Medicare.

He opposes health care for every American

and supports giving the wealthy more tax breaks.

Scott Klug is leaning to the right,

and for most voters in southern Wisconsin,

too far to the right.

(A man falls off his chair.)

Let's elect a congressman who leans a little more in our direction.

Tom Hecht, Congress

Tom told me that "Madison was very progressive, but maybe the rest of the district was a little more conservative than we thought." He was also outspent four to one, and the voters in his district and state did, in fact, lean to the right. Winning a Clio provided some consolation.

39

DIRTY LAUNDRY

The 2002 New Orleans mayoral race was a wild affair. Fifteen candidates were running in the primary. Unless someone got fifty percent of the vote, a runoff election would be held between the top two candidates.

The three leading candidates were Ray Nagin, a pro-business reformer and political outsider, Richard Pennington, the police superintendent, and Paulette Irons, a state senator. Candidate Troy Carter, a city councilman, figured that in order to make the runoff, he needed to leap past Paulette Irons.

Nagin received the endorsement of the *Times-Picayune* and was heading into the runoff. Carter needed to act quickly and forcefully. I got a call from one of his supporters who gave me "the dirt" on Irons and asked me to make an ad attacking her.

Irons was running as a reformer and anti-patronage candidate, but apparently, she had a long and well-documented history of political patronage as a state senator. And during her campaign, she tried to get sympathy for the death of her brother, but failed to mention that he was killed while robbing a grocery store.

We assembled a funky cast of New Orleans characters and let them tell the story. Here are the script and still frames:

"Dirty Laundry" 30-sec. TV

(Reporter) This is where Paulette Irons brings her dirty laundry.

What did you see in there?

(Woman) Some real dirty laundry.

(Man) I saw two jobs at taxpayer expense.

(Woman) That's some dirty laundry!

(Man) A 49 thousand dollar contract Paulette got for her best friend.

(Woman) 115 thousand dollars in state contracts for her political consultants.

(Man) Money from an elected official with no public disclosure.

(Reporter) And there you have it folks. Paulette Irons' dirty laundry.

(Woman) Hey, this gonna be on TV?

Paulette Irons did not make the runoff. Neither did Troy Carter. Ray Nagin was elected mayor and served two four-year terms. And speaking of dirty laundry, after leaving office, Nagin was convicted on twenty of twenty-one charges of wire fraud, bribery, and how fitting, money laundering. He is currently in the big house serving a ten-year sentence.

Dirty little secrets
Dirty little lies
We got our dirty little fingers in everybody's pie.
We love to cut you down to size.
We love dirty laundry.

– "Dirty Laundry" by Don Henley

40

SALON DES REFUSÉS

Rejection hurts. Dr. Guy Winch, a psychologist, writes that "MRI studies show that the same areas of the brain become activated when we experience rejection as when we experience physical pain. This is why rejection hurts so much (neurologically speaking)." He also points out that rejection can cause feelings of anger and aggression, "Countless studies have demonstrated that even mild rejections lead people to take out their aggression on innocent bystanders."

I never felt like taking out my aggression on innocent bystanders. And truth be told, the aggression quickly dissolved into lament, a feeling of sorrow for an idea DOA – an idea that the client just didn't understand, appreciate, want to pay for or have the money to pay for. In some cases, these scripts were actually also-rans – concepts that were considered, but rejected in favor of others. These stillborn creations were lovingly laid to rest in the Salon des Refusés, where they could, at some later date, be resurrected for future clients.

The Salon des Refusés, ("exhibition of rejects") refers to the Paris Salon of 1863 sponsored by the French government and the Academy of Fine Arts. In that year, two-thirds of the paintings presented were refused. The rejected artists appealed to Emperor Napoleon III, who was sensitive to public opinion. The Emperor's office issued a statement:

"His Majesty, wishing to let the public judge the legitimacy of these complaints, has decided that the works of art which were refused should be displayed in another part of the

Palace of Industry."

Hence, the Salon des Refusés, which attracted more than a thousand visitors a day.

My Salon gets only one visitor – me – whenever I suffer writer's block or just need a good idea right away. So, welcome to the Salon. The gallery of works on the following pages include some of my favorite rejections.

"Melancholy Baby" 30-sec. TV

(Music in background: "Melancholy Baby")

(Forlorn woman sitting at bar. Bartender leans in.)

(Bartender) Why so melancholy baby?

(Woman) Broken heart.

(Bartender) Oh my, who did this to you?

(Woman) My congressman.

(Bartender) What happened?

(Woman) I really liked this guy. Helped him get re-elected. Now he says he's going to vote to cut federal funding for hospital care.

(Bartender) Sorry baby.

(Woman) And that means fewer doctors and nurses.

(Hospital scene with doctor, nurses and patient)

Longer waits for care.

(Patients sitting in hospital waiting room)

Closing trauma centers.

(Emergency room scene)

(Bartender) Wow, that's tough. Anything I can do for you baby?

(Woman) Yeah, there's one thing.

(Bartender) What's that?

(Woman) Stop calling me baby.

(Super: Protect Medicare and Medicaid)

"Regulator" 60-sec. Radio

(Sound of doorbell, door opening)

(Homeowner) Yes?

(Regulator) Hello, I'm the cable regulator guy.

(Homeowner) You mean, the regular cable guy?

(Regulator) No, the cable regulator guy. I'm here to regulate the cable company.

(Homeowner, confused) Wait a minute, you're not the

regular cable guy?

(Regulator) Well, I am the regular cable regulator guy.

(Homeowner) The what?

(Announcer) Here in Montgomery County, thousands of people enjoy high-speed internet service from their cable company. This has spurred competition, encouraged innovation and lowered prices. If we regulate the internet service, we will restrict technological competition, limit consumer choice and risk higher prices. On behalf of the many consumers, businesses, schools and libraries who enjoy this low-cost service, we have this message for those in government: Let's not regulate the cable company. Instead, let's encourage fair competition and keep freedom of choice.

(Homeowner) So now, what is it you're trying to regulate?

(Regulator) Sir, please, I'm from the government and I'm here to help you.

"Ne Touchez Pas" 60-sec. Radio

(Noisy bar sounds, music)

(Man) Hello there, I'm Bob.

(Woman, in French accent) Ne touchez pas, Monsieur.

(Man) Uh, pardon me?

(Woman) Hands off, Mister.

(Man) But miss, I had no intention of...

(Woman) You are wiz ze government, no?

(Man) Yes, but...

(Woman) And you want your hands on ze cable company, no?

(Man) Well, yes, but only to regulate cable's high speed internet service.

(Woman) Monsieur Bob, ze cable company's internet service has created competition and lower prices for consumers.

(Man) Well, yes, but...

(Woman) And ze competition is good, no?

(Man) Yes.

(Woman) And ze lower prices are good too, no?

(Man) Well, I guess so.

(Woman) So why would you want to regulate zat which is good for business and good for consumers?

(Man) I guess you've got a point there.

(Announcer) Ne touchez pas means hands-off, and that means more choice for consumers and more competition among the various technologies that give the residents of Montgomery County high-speed internet access. Without regulation, all technologies can compete freely in the open marketplace, benefiting all consumers. Let's encourage freedom of choice and fair competition. Let's keep hands-off the cable company.

(Woman) So, Monsieur Bob, ne touchez pas is good, no?

(Man) Uh, well, yes, maybe it is good.

(Woman) Très bien, Monsieur Bob.

(Sound of glasses clinking)

And now, laissez le bons temp roullier.

(Man) Uh, pardon me?

"DJ" 30-sec. TV

(DJ and girlfriend in old radio station studio)

(Ending music and vocal) …the worst I ever had.

(DJ) Great ol' song, "The Best You Ever Gave Me Was the Worst I Ever Had." Kinda sums up Charlie Foti's record as sheriff. I mean, in Foti's jail, people got beat up, abused, denied health care, plus all those illegal strip searches that cost the citizens of Orleans Parish millions of dollars. And now he wants his old job back. Listen up, Charlie, I'm gonna dedicate this next song to you. That good ol' country tune, "All I Want from You Is Away."

(Music and vocal) All I want from you is away…

(Photo of Marlin Gusman)

(VO announcer) Re-elect Sheriff Marlin Gusman.

"Wally" 30-sec. TV

(Stand-up comedian on stage)

(Comedian) Hey, did you hear about this guy, Wally Rothschild running for judge? First he was a Democrat, then he became a Republican, and now he switched back to Democrat. Could you imagine this guy as a judge?

"I find the defendant innocent…I mean guilty…no, make that innocent."

(Laughter, rim shot)

Oh, and get this, Rothschild *reduced* the charges on dozens of felony cases. "Let's see, you killed ten people with a meat ax because you had a bad hair day. Oh poor fellow. Why don't I just reduce that charge to a misdemeanor.

(Audience groans, rim shot)

I mean, what *is* this guy, an idiot? You put criminals in jail. Didn't he get the memo?

(Laughter)

(Super: Anne Marie Vandenweghe, District Judge)

(VO announcer) Anne Marie Vandenweghe, District Judge

"Congressman" 30-sec. TV

(Arrogant congressman at a town hall meeting surrounded by angry constituents)

(Congressman) Folks, we need to cut two hundred billion dollars in Medicare and Medicaid payments to hospitals.

Now I know that as a result, a lot of you might not get the hospital care you need, but please don't call me, I'm not a doctor, I'm a congressman, and I'm sorry if you and your families get hurt, but we've just gotta make these cuts.

And frankly, I'm sure all of you will understand.

(A constituent approaches him.)

(Congressman) Yes?

(Constituent, sarcastically) Frankly congressman, we *don't* understand.

(Congressman looks stunned and insulted.)

(Super: Protect Medicare and Medicaid)

(VO announcer) Tell Congress to protect Medicare and Medicaid.

"Operating Room" 30-sec. TV

(A team of surgeons and nurses are working on a patient in

an operating suite. Quick cuts to close-ups of faces, hands, equipment)

(Doctor) Good work team. Our patient is going to be just fine.

(Suddenly, a heavy-set, middle-aged man in a suit holding a clipboard bursts into the room.)

(Man) Excuse me, I'm from the government and we need to cut four billion dollars in Medicare and Medicaid payments to hospitals.

(Cut to nurse.)

(Nurse) How did you get in here?

(Cut to man.)

(Man) We've got to cut spending, so come on folks, let's wrap this up!

(Cut to doctor.)

(Doctor) Jimmy, call security!

(Patient sits up from operating table. Looks bewildered.)

(Cut to on-camera narrator in hospital corridor.)

(Narrator to camera) If Congress cuts billions of dollars in federal funding to hospitals, that could overload emergency rooms, shut down trauma units and reduce patient access to the latest treatments.

Let's not cut Medicare and Medicaid payments to hospitals. It's bad medicine, bad politics and bad for America.

(Cut back to operating suite, where two burly security guards are about to escort the "man from the government" out the door.)

(Super: Protect Medicare and Medicaid)

"Travel Agent" 30-sec. TV

(Smiling man in suit with briefcase walking toward camera on crowded airport concourse)

(VO announcer) This is a bureaucrat from the U.S. Department of Transportation and he's your new travel agent.

(Cut to woman screaming from old horror movie.)

(Dramatic shot of airplane taking off. Animated graphic showing 36% decline in average airfares.)

The average airplane ticket has dropped 36 percent since deregulation, which means more people can afford to fly to more places than ever before.

(Scene from old religious movie – worshippers kneeling on ground with arms raised toward the sky shouting "Hallelujah!!")

(Scenes of bureaucrat in a variety of scenes where he appears to be ridiculous, unneeded and meddlesome – at ticket counter, baggage check-in, just standing in the middle of the concourse eating a big pretzel)

But bureaucrats from the Department of Transportation want to re-regulate the airline industry, which will cost air travellers time and money.

(Peter Lorre from old movie, "I'm going to kill him!")

(Bureaucrat seated at desk, smiling at camera, doing nothing)

The last thing we need is a government bureaucrat who dreams of being a travel agent.

(Footage of comedian Jack Benny, "This is ridiculous!")

(Dramatic shot of airplane in flight)

Let's keep deregulation working. Anything else won't fly.

(Super: Deregulation. Anything else won't fly.)

(Super: A message from the Air Transport Association)

"I Can Fix It." 30-sec. TV

(Open on D.O.T. bureaucrat, coat and tie, wearing tool belt around his waist. His is dragging a long ladder and walks hurriedly on an airport tarmac toward a jet airplane parked at gate. The sight is ludicrous. A normal looking guy walks along beside him. They are animated and arguing.)

(Bureaucrat) I can fix it.

(Man) But it's not broken!

(Bureaucrat) Doesn't matter. I can fix it.

(Man) But it's not broken!!!

(Bureaucrat) Look, I'm from the government and I'm here to fix it.

(Medium wide shot of bureaucrat climbing up tall ladder against jet engine. He has a huge plumber's wrench in his hand. Ground crew and baggage handlers are gathering around the scene.)

(VO announcer) Bureaucrats at the Department of Transportation think they need to fix the airline industry through regulation. Perhaps they don't realize that the average price of an airline ticket has gone down 36 percent since deregulation 20 years ago.

(Bureaucrat leans his head into jet engine)

(Shot of bureaucrat from POV of passengers in airplane)

(Bureaucrat with tire iron at tire of landing gear)

(Bureaucrat walking on wing with big drill in hand)

(VO announcer) We don't need to fix something that's not broken. Let's keep deregulation.

(Man, sarcastically shouting up to bureaucrat on wing)

(Man) So did you fix it?

(Bureaucrat) Don't bother me, I'm busy.

(Rack focus and super: Deregulation. If it ain't broke...)

(Sound of power drill, metal crashing sounds, siren)

(Super: A message from the Air Transport Association)

"Bad Propositions" 30-sec. TV

(Crowded bar. An attractive woman is seated at bar, surrounded by several men.)

(Super: Bad Propositions)

(First guy) Hey baby, how 'bout a ride on the ol' Harley?

(She rolls her eyes. Picture flips.)

(Second guy) Another Courvoisier for the lady?

(She ignores him. Picture flips.)

(Third guy) I'm a movie producer and I thought maybe you and I...

(She takes a deep breath.)

(Cut to bartender. He shakes his head as though he's heard these lines a million times.)

(VO announcer) Bad propositions usually don't get far.

(Picture flips.)

(Fourth guy) So that's why I'm proposing that we re-regulate the airline industry.

(Woman shakes her head.)

(Scenes of airports and airlines)

(VO announcer) Re-regulating the airline industry is a bad proposition. The average ticket price has dropped 36 percent since deregulation, which means that more people can afford to fly to more places than ever before.

(Fifth guy) Can I...

(Woman) No thank you.

(VO announcer) Say no thank you to bad propositions. Keep deregulation working.

(Super: Keep Deregulation Working)

(Super: A message from the Air Transport Association)

"Conscience" 30-sec. TV

(Older man with grey beard in white limbo wearing white suit, bolo tie, panama hat)

(Slow zoom in to medium close-up)

Hello Charlie, it's me, your conscience.

I hope you listen to me Charlie, because you're not telling the whole truth.

People died in your jail Charlie. People were beaten, abused and denied healthcare. Plus you cost the people of New Orleans ten million dollars because you illegally strip-searched minor traffic offenders.

Listen to me Charlie. Listen to your conscience and tell the truth, the whole truth.

(Super: Re-elect Marin Gusman, Sheriff)

"What Where You Thinking?" 30-sec. TV

(Music, game show set)

(Host) It's America's favorite game show, "What Were You Thinking? Our first question goes to Congressman Bill Bunkmeister.

(Congressman) BANKmeister!

(Host) Congressman, what were you thinking when you proposed cutting billions of dollars for Medicare hospital funding?

(Congressman) Well frankly...

(Host) Well frankly Congressman, you *weren't* thinking because these cuts are going to hurt a lot of people.

(Congressman) But I...

(Host) But you what, congressman? You didn't think it would hurt families all across America?

(Congressman) The American people...

(Host) The American people *support* funding for healthcare, congressman. What were you thinking?

(VO announcer) Tell Congress what *you* think. Do not cut funding for hospital care.

(Super: Protect Medicare and Medicaid)

"Bonehead Idea" 30-sec. TV

(Cheesy stage set. Male MC in shiny tuxedo holding trophy, female MC in low-cut dress)

(Super: The 2013 Bonehead Awards)

(MC man) And this year's Bonehead Award for the dumbest idea in government goes to...

(Drum roll)

(MC woman) Congressman Rodney Flackenbacker!

(Mild applause)

(Recipient walks on stage, accepts Bonehead trophy, approaches microphone and starts thanking people.)

(Various camera angles on recipient. Cutaways to smiling

MCs and audience. Star filters, light flares, kitsch galore)

(Congressman) Yes, it was my idea - cut 4 billion dollars in Medicare and Medicaid payments to hospitals.

(MC woman) Which if passed, could result in overcrowding, fewer nurses, longer waits and reduced quality of patient care.

(Congressman) Right, but we've got to make cuts somewhere. Thank you very much!

(Congressman holds trophy in air.)

(Scant applause, a few boos)

(VO announcer) Cutting federal funding for hospitals. A real bonehead idea.

(Super: Protect Medicare and Medicaid)

"What?" 30-sec. TV

(Poet on stage)

Some don't care if it is Medicare.
They want to make a cut which makes me say what?
Cut four billion dollars to hospitals in federal funding?
I was just wondering if cutting Medicare and Medicaid
payments to hospitals is good for America?
What do you think? How do you feel?
Should we let Congress think it's enabled
to hurt seniors, the poor and disabled?
Does the mandate of a plurality last year

mean we should abandon morality this year?
What do you think? How do you feel?
Some don't care if it is Medicare.
They want to make a cut which makes me say what?
Call your member of Congress and say
What, what are you thinking?
Please don't cut federal funding for the hospitals of
America.

(Super: Protect Medicare and Medicaid)

"Joke" 30-sec. TV

(Comedian on stage) Hey there, I'm a comedian. Sometimes I make jokes at other people's expense, and so does Congress.

They say they want to help you by cutting Medicare and Medicaid for hospitals. What a joke, but not funny, unless you think a do-it-yourself triple bypass is funny.

(Laughter)

If we let Congress get away with cutting funding for hospital care, then the joke's on us. So let's send Congress a message – do not cut Medicare and Medicaid funding for hospital care.

And please, leave the jokes to the professionals. Thank you.

(Applause)

(Super: Protect Medicare and Medicaid)

"Answerman" 30-sec. TV

(Wonkish man sitting at desk wearing headphones. Pocket protector in shirt pocket with lots of pens. Laptop, telephone, stacks of books and papers on desk)

(VO announcer) It's time to ask the Answerman!

(Canned applause)

(Answerman punches button on phone before taking each call.)

(Answerman) Answerman.

(Caller #1) Is Y2K gonna be a problem?

(Answerman) Y2K's not the problem. It's the frivolous lawsuits that come later.

Answerman.

(Caller #2) Yo Answerman!

(Answerman) Yo.

(Caller #2) Who's going to pay for these frivolous lawsuits?

(Answerman) You and me pal.

Answerman.

(Caller #3) I just love your show!

(Answerman) That's not a question.

Answerman.

(Caller #4) So what'll we do now, Answerman?

(Answerman) Stop the lawsuits before they happen.

Answerman.

(Caller #5) Honey, don't forget the milk and bread.

(Answerman) Yes dear.

(Answerman to camera) Thank you and good night.

(Canned applause)

(Answerman removes headphones and walks off camera.)

(VO announcer) Answerman is a presentation of your local Chamber of Commerce.

(Super: Y2K. No Frivolous Lawsuits)

"Crystal Ball" 30-sec. TV

(The scene is the parlor of a fortune teller – a mysterious woman wearing a head wrap, blouse with puff sleeves, lots of jewelry and heavy makeup. She is sitting at a table gazing into a crystal ball. A male business executive is seated across from her.)

(Music: gypsy theme)

(Executive) So what does Y2K look like?

(Fortune teller) It looks like we'll solve the problem.

(Executive) No bugs, no glitches?

(Fortune teller) I see a few disruptions.

(Executive) Like what?

(Fortune teller) Greed and avarice.

(Executive) Hey, I know those guys! What else?

(Fortune teller) I see frivolous lawsuits.

(Executive) Yeah, vulture city.

(Fortune teller) But I see hope.

(Executive) Hope for what?

(Fortune teller) For the consumers of America. If we enact meaningful reforms dealing with these frivolous lawsuits, then the consumers won't get stuck paying the bill.

(Executive) So what do we do?

(Fortune teller) We support measures that preempt state and local liability, provide incentives for corporate community engagement, and pass laws that offer protection from frivolous lawsuits.

(Executive) How do you know all this?

(Fortune teller) I have an MBA from Stanford.

(Super: Y2K. No Frivolous Lawsuits)

"The Studio" 60-sec. Radio

(Studio sound engineer) OK, this'll be take three.

(Excited, over-modulated announcer) Good news, folks! Now you can be a local hero when you buy locally grown food and farm products.

(Sound of studio door opening, footsteps)

(Ad man) I'm from the ad agency and I'm here to help you promote local farmers.

(Announcer #1) But I don't need help. I'm a professional!

(Ad man) Congratulations. Now read this script.

(Announcer #1) But, who are all these people?

(Sounds of people shuffling into studio, banging and clanging sounds)

(Ad man) This is the band. That's the choir.

(Announcer #1) Band? Choir?

(Ad man) Trust me. Just read the script.

(Engineer) Take four.

(Announcer #1) Good news, folks...

(Hallelujah chorus from Handel's "Messiah")

(Announcer #1) You can be a local hero…

(Big musical fanfare)

(Announcer #1) when you buy locally grown food and farm products at your neighborhood grocery store.

(Musical flourish)

(Announcer #1) This is ridiculous!

(Ad man) This is show biz!

(Announcer #1) I'm calling my agent!

(Announcer #2) No matter how you tell the story, the fact is that local farmers are your neighbors, and here in western Massachusetts, they're committed to growing the healthiest foods, protecting the environment and preserving a quality of life that's endured in our communities for hundreds of years. That makes them heroes too. So won't you be a local hero? Just look for the "local hero" label where you shop.

(Ad man) Please, just try this one line.

(Announcer #1) Feel good about yourself, buy locally grown food and farm products.

(James Brown vocal) I feel good!!

(Announcer) Now that's not bad.

(Ad man) I knew you'd like it.

(Announcer #2) A message from CISA, Community Involved In Sustaining Agriculture

"Patient" 15-sec. TV

(Patient in hospital bed. He seems agitated. Nurse is checking his IV.)

(VO announcer) Meet Fred Butkus, a hospital patient who's lost his patience.

(Butkus) That's right. I've lost my patience with Congress. They want to cut Medicare for hospitals!

(Nurse) Calm down, Mr. Butkus.

(Butkus) Makes me sick!

(Nurse) You're already sick.

(Butkus) Gimme that phone. I'm calling my congressman.

(He reaches for phone.)

(VO announcer) Lost your patience with Congress? Log on and we'll show you what to do.

(Super: Protect Medicare and Medicaid)

"Broken Hearts" 30-sec. TV

(An 8-piece band is on stage playing an instrumental version of "Sergeant Pepper's Lonely Hearts Club Band." A large broken heart is on each of the music stands. On-screen documentation is shown during each band member's comment.)

(Music - "Sergeant Pepper's Lonely Hearts Club Band")

(Open on band playing.)

(VO announcer) Introducing the Paulette Irons Broken Hearts Club Band.

(Cut away to individual band member interviews.)

(Band member #1) Paulette broke my heart when she changed her mind about patronage.

(Band member #2) She broke my heart when she got a 300 thousand dollar state contract for one of her political cronies.

(Band member #3) The ethics violation for double dipping – that's what broke my heart.

(Band member #4) A 35 thousand dollar kickback for giving a local judge a cash contribution. Now that's heartbreaking.

(Wide shot of band on stage)

(VO announcer) Don't let Paulette Irons break your heart.

(Band member #5 to camera) Paulette, when you broke my heart, you lost my vote.

"Fly" 30-sec. TV

(Open on Paulette Irons' office. Camera (steadicam) weaves around the office trying to find a fly that is noisily buzzing around.)

(The camera POV is that of a person trying to kill the fly. At several points during the spot, an arm is seen holding a fly swatter. The arm swats at the fly but always misses.)

(On-screen documentation is shown for each charge against Irons.)

(VO fly) Hiya doin'? I'm a fly on da wall in Paulette Irons' office and I've seen it all!

She's been double dippin' at taxpayer expense takin' her legislative salary plus another salary from her buddy, the recorder of mortgages.

She got a 300 thousand dollar state contract for a friend.

Gets 35 thousand dollars a year in legal fees from a local judge to whom she gave a cash contribution.

And now she's got an ethics violation pending against her.

Look pal, I'm just a fly on da wall. Check it out yourself. You don't need eyes on da back of your head to see what

Paulette Irons been up to.

(Super: Paid for by Friends of Troy Carter)

"Hall of Shame" 30-sec. TV

(United States Capitol)

(Dissolve to camera dolly of photographic portraits hanging on wall. The photos are of political leaders of dubious distinction – Richard Nixon, Spiro Agnew, Huey Long and Frank Riggs.)

(Music and vocal: "Ain't That a Shame")

(VO announcer) This is the Congressional Hall of Shame, and this is former Congressman Frank Riggs' shameful record.

(Camera dollies portraits to reveal Frank Riggs.)

(Slow zoom into photo of Riggs. Rack focus and super his voting record with documentation.)

Riggs voted to cut funding for education.

He voted against the family and medical leave act.

He voted against banning assault weapons, against job training programs, against Medicaid and senior citizens benefits.

(Photo of Riggs comes back into focus.)

Send Frank Riggs back to Congress??

(Music and vocal) Ain't that a shame.

(VO announcer) That would be a shame.

(Dissolve to photo of Dan Hamburg.)

"Eyes and Ears" 30-sec. TV

(Open on close-up of actor standing on sidewalk. He is wearing large blinders obscuring his peripheral vision and is holding his index fingers in his ears. His eyes are shut tightly. Documentation appears on lower third of screen.)

(VO announcer #1) Did you see that big Harley Chief Pennington got as a gift from a city contractor?

(Man) Didn't see it.

(VO announcer #1) Did you hear about those contraband guns that wound up back on the streets after the chief decided to trade them instead of destroying them?

(Man) Didn't hear it.

(VO announcer #1) Did you see the chief out campaigning at taxpayer expense for the mayor's third term?

(Man) Missed it.

(VO announcer #1) Have you heard about the chief protecting his retirement benefits while running for mayor, Again at taxpayer expense?

(Man) Didn't hear a thing.

(VO announcer #2) Open your eyes and ears. Chief Pennington may be a decent man, but he's got very poor judgment.

(VO announcer #1) Have you seen the new panda bear at the Audubon Zoo?

(Man) Is that a trick question?

(Super: Paid for by Friends of Troy Carter)

"Boom, Boom" 60-sec. Radio

(Children's chorus singing the popular children's song, "Boom, Boom, Ain't It Great To Be Crazy")

(Children's chorus)
Boom, boom ain't it great to be crazy.
Boom, boom ain't it great to be crazy.
Giddy and foolish the whole day through.
Boom, boom ain't it great to be crazy.

(Music under announcer)

(Announcer) Sometimes, children like to act silly and foolish, but when our state legislators act like that, it can cost you, the taxpayers, a lot of money. Several of our lawmakers have come up with a crazy idea. They want to pass an oil and gas processing tax which, they claim, will help our state. But that's a lot of foolishness. Economists and newspapers all across the state have joined with a majority of the legislature in opposing this tax which could raise the cost of gasoline by 25 cents a gallon, increase our utility rates, eliminate jobs and hurt the economy. That's why a majority of voters also oppose this tax, which has already been killed three times in the legislature. The oil and gas processing tax...a crazy idea.

(Children's chorus) Boom, boom ain't it great to be crazy.

(Announcer) A message from the Alliance for a Strong Louisiana Economy

"Bureau vs. Bureaucrat" 30-sec. TV

(John Cleese on camera. On his right is a beautiful antique bureau. On his left is a heavy-set, older male in a suit staring into space.)

(Cleese on camera. Points to bureau then bureaucrat)

This is a bureau. This is a bureaucrat.

A bureau will take your shirts and socks.

A bureaucrat will take the shirt off your back and sock it to you.

Currently, there is a bill in the United States Senate, the McCain bill, that is well-intentioned, but short-sighted. It will create 17 new federal boards, commissions, panels and task forces, not to mention 500 of these (points to bureaucrat) at a cost to you, the taxpayer, of 200 million dollars.

(The bureaucrat casts a wary eye at Cleese, who walks over to the bureau, puts a hand on it while grabbing his shirt with the other hand.)

If the McCain bill passes, ladies and gentlemen, lock your drawers and hang on to your shirts.

(Super: A Message from the National Association of Convenience Stores)

"Feel the Heat" 30-sec. TV

(Congressman seated behind desk in office. He's all full of himself.)

(Congressman to camera) I'm a congressman. Just got re-elected. Now I can vote to cut federal funding for hospital care and not worry about the 80 percent of Americans who support Medicare and Medicaid.

Look, I'm sorry if these cuts will inconvenience a few million people, but hey, we've all got to make sacrifices.

So please, don't bother calling or writing. I'm here for two more years, and as Clark Gable would say, "Frankly my dear, I don't give a da..." (bleep)

(VO announcer) For those in Congress who don't see the light, let's make them feel the heat. Log on to our website to learn how you can protect funding for hospital care.

(Super: Protect Medicare and Medicaid)

"Bad" 30-sec. TV

(Point of view looking through peephole of door. Extreme wide angle shot of a man and a woman looking through the peephole. They knock on door.)

(Knock, knock)

(Woman) Austin Badon! We know you're in there.

(Man) You got some explaining to do!

(Knock, knock)

(Woman leans into peephole. Her face is comically distorted by wide-angle lens.)

(Woman) You're bad, Austin.

(Man) You're bad on ethics.

(Woman) You took money from a lobbyist for a trip to Washington that you never reported.

(Man) Bad on women.

(Woman) You voted against planned parenthood.

(Man) Bad on teachers.

(Woman) You voted against employer payments to the teacher retirement fund.

(Man) Bad on the environment.

(Woman) You voted to phase out solar energy subsidies.

(Man) Bad on crime.

(Woman) You voted against making concealed handgun permits public record.

(Knock, knock)

(Man leans into peephole.)

(Man) Austin Badon!

(Woman) You're bad on everything!

(VO announcer) Timothy Ray, clerk of court.

And that concludes the exhibition of works in the Salon des Refusés. I hope you enjoyed the tour and the book. If you'd like to see some of the ads described in this book, please go to denoseder.com.

ACKNOWLEDGMENTS

Thank you to my family who served in various roles in my productions (Jonathan – production designer; Veronica – actor, researcher and production assistant; Julie, actor and voice talent; Dorothy – associate producer; Jutka, Alex and Joshua – actors). Special thanks to my son and partner Jeorge who co-produced, directed and edited many of the ads and videos described in this book.

Film and video production is a collaborative craft. I depend on the talents and skills of many people to help make the finished product. Thank you to all my actors and actresses, crew members, set and production designers, narrators, casting agencies, technicians, researchers and other collaborators. Special thanks to the people behind the camera who brought my scripts to life – Glenn Pearcy, Bob Ipcar, Scott Lloyd-Davies, Jeffrey Kimble, Tom Buckholtz, Ken Morrison, Stanley Staniski, George Rosenberg, Erich Roland, Randy DeLeo, Bob Perrin, Paul Young, Jamie Sides, Troy Dick, Tom Kaufman, Gary Grieg, Francis James, Richard Chisholm and Peter Mullet, to name a few.

Thanks to Victor Rook, who expertly formatted this book and guided me through the publishing process.

I give a big shout-out of appreciation to my many clients over the years who read and approved my scripts and allowed me to inject a little wit and humor in their media campaigns.

And finally, my heartfelt gratitude and love to my wife, creative partner, art director and book editor, Anita Semjen, who has always forced me to write and rewrite until I got it right.

Made in the USA
Middletown, DE
21 July 2019